"Only consummate Florida outdoor writer Doug Alderson could have penned such a delightful - and practical - guide to exploring the state's natural wonders. From the south's Florida Keys to the northwest's Blackwater River and dozens of points in between, Alderson has paddled, hiked, mapped and come to intimately know the hidden treasures of the Sunshine State. We are all lucky that his gift of storytelling and research allows us to join him on adventures that teach, enlighten and inspire others to become stewards of the always vulnerable, but still magical land that is Florida."
    Jennifer Portman, *Tallahassee Democrat* senior writer.

"I've had a great time traipsing around the Florida rivers and trails with Doug Alderson, and as a Florida native, I learn something new every trip. I'm very excited about this book... so I can help unlock the secret places Doug knows about and I haven't been!"
    Bryan Desloge, President, Florida Association of Counties

"With a naturalist's keen eye and the sense of adventure of an explorer, Doug Alderson reveals a compelling glimpse of Florida. Wild Florida Adventures *proves that there's so much more to the Sunshine State than condos and theme parks. Let Alderson be your guide in exploring his favorite parts of Florida, the primeval places where time stands still."*
    Conor Mihel, editor-at-large, *Canoe & Kayak* Magazine

Wild Florida Adventures

Exploring the Sunshine State by Land and Water

Doug Alderson

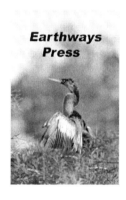

Copyright 2014 by Doug Alderson
All rights reserved

www.dougalderson.net

ISBN-10: 1497425824
ISBN-13: 978-1497425828

Earthways Press
960 Towhee Road
Tallahassee, FL 32305

Cover photo: Chris Robertson paddles past giant cypress knees in Sutton's Lake off the Apalachicola River.

All photos by Doug Alderson unless otherwise stated

To all of my adventure companions, past and present.

Apalachicola RiverTrek group, 2012

Table of Contents

Regional maps		1
Foreword		5
1.	The Florida Keys Challenge	8
2.	Peace among Mangroves at Weedon Island	20
3.	Titusville's Magical Glowing Waters	26
4.	On Being a Lunatic	31
5.	When You Need a Guide: Paddling the Thousand Islands	36
6.	The Wekiva Promise	40
7.	Devilish Limpkins and Seminole Echoes on the Withlacoochee South	50
8.	Fishy Business on the Econlockhatchee	64
9.	The Santa Fe's Naked Man	68
10.	Paddling the Low and Slow River of Song	78
11.	Revisiting Rock Island	83
12.	The Wacissa's Last Limpkin	87
13.	Paddling among Giants	93
14.	Florida's Remotest Spot	99
15.	Onward, to the Pinhook!	105
16.	Night of the Attacking Mullet	109
17.	Bringing Back the Holy Grail of Springs?	112
18.	Paddling the Swift Ochlockonee from Dam to the Bay	119
19.	100,000 Paddle Strokes on the Thirsty Apalachicola	126
20.	Devon Creek Magic	138
21.	Dry Creek Sunday	140

22.	Panhandle Perfection	143
23.	Bedouin Kayaking	146
24.	North Florida's Botanical Eden	159
25.	The Great Bradwell Bay Swamp Hike	168
26.	Hiking the Aucilla Wilds	174
27.	Where Wilderness Takes Over	180
28.	Racing Mosquitoes at Wakulla State Forest	189
29.	Restoration Beginnings at St. Sebastian	192
30.	Fakahatchee Strand: North America's Amazon	201
31.	Camping with the He-Coon	208
32.	Cave Camping	216
33.	When Plans Go Awry: Tackling the Mighty Mississippi	221
34.	Becoming Curmudgeonly about Life Jackets	232
35.	Florida Spirit	238
	Bibliography	240
	Index	245

A hiker walks through a wet corridor in the Bradwell Bay Wilderness of Florida's Apalachicola National Forest.

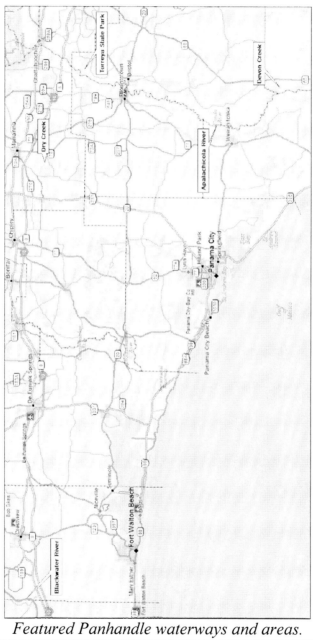

Featured Panhandle waterways and areas.

Featured Big Bend waterways and areas.

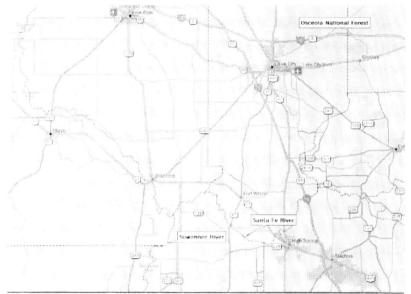

Featured North-central Florida waterways and areas.

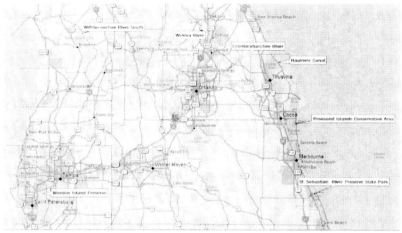

Featured Central Florida waterways and areas.

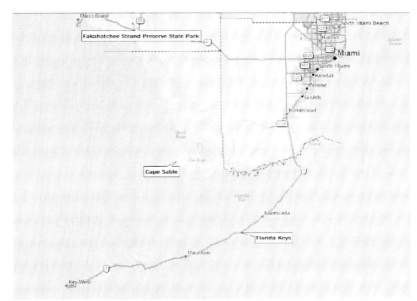
Featured South Florida waterways and areas.

Preening great egret along the Wakulla River.

Foreword

As a younger adult who traveled the country quite a bit, my notable days in the outdoors were mostly out West or in the Appalachians—hiking New Hampshire's Franconia Ridge on a clear day with panoramic views on all sides, scaling a Colorado peak, walking the Continental Divide in Glacier National Park amidst a profusion of wildflowers and tumbling cascades of water from melting snow. "This is the best day of my life!" I've exclaimed on more than one occasion.

Increasingly, however, my memorable outings are in Florida. It is usually when humidity has fallen, bugs are sparse, and I've joined friends or family on a hiking or paddling trip. It could be cruising past limestone walls on the Suwannee, exploring the Keys, Ten Thousand Islands or Big Bend Coast, gliding through the wild canopy of the Wacissa Slave Canal, slogging through a pristine swamp, or hiking Torreya State Park in spring with the scent of magnolia blossoms in the air.

Sometimes, it is embarking on an outing with a purpose. I often help to organize and participate in the annual five-day Apalachicola RiverTrek in mid-October on the Apalachicola River. Air is usually crisp, the river beautiful, current swift, and the company outstanding. We also spread awareness about the plight of Apalachicola Bay and raise needed funds for the Apalachicola Riverkeeper. Having fun while supporting a cause—a dynamite combination!

A perfect outing is a natural high. If camping, dreams seem more profound. The very earth and water feels alive, and I have a strong sense of gratitude.

Do the blissful feelings last? How could they? We return to a world where work must be done, bills must be paid, and life's challenges confront us. Perfect outings are select windows. The feelings and sensations may return some day, but the exact circumstances will not. That's why they feel so special when they occur. We can carry part of them with us; they can help us through the not-so-good days. And their memories prompt us to plan the next adventure.

In this volume, I describe a few perfect Florida outings, but also some imperfect ones. Perhaps we learn more lessons from the "character building" adventures, often as a result of poor planning, and we can have a hearty laugh in retrospect.

These stories are mostly about adventures in a kayak, and I revisit a couple of favorite places described in my previous book, *Wild Florida Waters,* but with a different twist. I've also added a few unique accounts of land adventures. Some are short takes, just long enough to inspire your own adventure, while the multi-day trips tend to be longer. Early versions of a couple of chapters were published in *Florida Wildlife* and *American Forests* magazines, and they have been updated for this book.

Additionally, a shorter version of "The Santa Fe's Naked Man" was a second place winner in the 2012 Red Hills Writing Contest for literary nonfiction.

I've even added one out-of-state adventure—trying to tackle the mighty Mississippi River by canoe—because it reveals the shortcomings of planning a long-distance trip a thousand miles away while in Florida. And being overly ambitious by utilizing untried theories. The results are disastrous—and funny.

On land or water, Florida is a wild playground because of its incredible beauty, diversity and vast stretches of public lands that have been so carefully protected. Let us strive to cherish and keep it, and make Florida better for those who follow.

Heart of Florida

Perhaps the heart of Florida is the combined energy of our physical and artistic expressions, natural and man-made beauty, even our innermost thoughts and prayers. And its essence is black and white, red, brown and yellow. It is also feathered and furred, scaled and smooth, leafed and sheathed with bark. It is clear, turbid and tannin-tinted. It is a pulse that goes out depleted of oxygen and nutrients and comes back refreshed, cleansed and inspired.

It is the heart of a land, something amorphous, something felt more than seen. And it will change, adjust, feel pain and be healed, but it will always remain strong as long as people feed it with fresh ideas and nurture it with love and respect... the heart of Florida.

1
The Florida Keys Challenge

"There are many wonderful glimpses of the sea that one obtains on a trip down over the Keys. One realizes this when the train slides off the mainland, down near Everglade, onto the first key, over an extenuated causeway. ... The Keys at times seem like emeralds in settings of silver floating on seas of lapis lazuli, and the soft trade winds sough through palm and mangrove and bay cedar."

>Nevin O. Winter, *Florida: The Land of Enchantment*, 1918

My timing was perfect. I joined the Paddle Florida Keys Challenge at Long Key State Park just after sunset as dinner was being served. "Hurry, get in line,

Doug!" group organizer Bill Richards shouted even before I stepped out of my car. I quickly joined a hungry procession of almost 70 paddlers and volunteers and learned of the trip's progress.

After a glass-calm opening stretch along Key Largo, the group encountered fierce winds and one paddler took an unscheduled swim. Still, spirits were high, cool weather was keeping bugs at bay, and no rain was in the immediate forecast. An unfettered panorama of stars soon shone across the vault of sky. That night, as a steady breeze rustled through palms, I lay in my tent in eager anticipation to begin paddling the remaining 78 miles to Key West, what the Spanish called Cayo Hueso—"Isle of Bones"—because the Spaniards found a number of human bones there.

On a chilly morning, we embarked on an 11-mile paddle to Curry Hammock State Park with a strong wind at our backs. This was my chance to re-accustom myself to ocean paddling since my recent multi-day trips had been on calm rivers. As we crossed the 2.5 mile stretch of open water at the Long Key Channel, paralleling 180 concrete arches of the historic Key West Railway Extension, waves kicked up to an irregular chop. They lifted up my bow and stern and rocked me from side to side. My legs shook a bit as they always do when first encountering rough water. Fear. It's natural.

In a kayak, fear must be faced by paddling and pausing at the right times and being firmly entrenched in the boat with thighs and hips. You need to feel confident in your craft, your skills, and your companions. As a back-up on this trip, we had the Coast Guard Auxiliary shadowing us in a small boat, so there was no need to worry. Plus, several paddlers were in radio contact with each other and, being the sweep boat, I had a radio.

More choppy waters greeted us on the way to Knight's Key the next day, but a lunch stop at Sombrero Beach couldn't have been better. Palm-lined with bright white sand, this was as tropical a beach as you could ask for, perfect for the many folks in our group from northern states. According to Bill, just less than half of our group was from Florida. Sixteen were from Michigan, seven from Georgia, three from Vermont, two from Alabama, two from New Jersey, two from Virginia, two from Tennessee and one each from Massachusetts, Maine, Montana, Oklahoma and West Virginia. January in sunny South Florida—who could ask for more?

Several scurrying iguanas added to the tropical flavor of Sombrero Beach, even though they are exotic pests that compete with native wildlife. The Florida Park Service is trying to rid them from the state parks, trapping hundreds. "Godzilla," a large iguana at Bahia Honda, was so named due to its ability to evade capture. It often perches regally on a high branch overlooking the Atlantic, protected from human intrusion by a thick buffer of sea grapes and other plants and shrubs. Park officials are prohibited from shooting the animal.

Sister's Creek sheltered us for the last three miles of our journey to the campground. Several paddlers branched off to explore thick mangrove tunnels in Boot Key while others occupied stools at the waterside Burdines bar and restaurant. The Keys are fun that way, offering diverse choices.

Busting my butt at the slippery launch at Knight's Key was the only thing that marred an otherwise perfect day for the Seven Mile Bridge crossing. Most of the surface was glass calm, the waters clear. The once choppy ocean became a giant aquarium. Bright orange Bahama starfish, stingrays, corals, sponges, sea grasses, fish and Portuguese man-of-war jellyfish could all be seen. Some of us explored historic Pigeon Key, once used as a base for railroad workers. The Florida Keys Challenge was being made on the centennial of Henry Flagler's Over-Sea Railroad reaching Key West in 1912, so railroad history had extra relevance. Eight century-old buildings on Pigeon Key are being well maintained for educational and historic purposes, and one houses the Railroad Museum. Several thousand men built the Florida Keys Over-Sea Railroad and our group would pass all twenty-three of the historic railroad bridges on the way to Key West.

  The most challenging bridge projects for Flagler were the Long Key Viaduct, Knights Key-Moser Channel Bridge (Seven-Mile Bridge), Bahia Honda Bridge, and the Key West Terminal. The Seven-Mile Bridge alone consisted of 546 concrete foundation piers—more than used at any bridge in the world at the time—210 53-foot arches, 335 80-foot and 60-foot deck plate steel spans, and a 253-foot drawbridge. Each pier built in the main channel for this span required enough sand, gravel, cement and other materials to fill the cargo hull of a five-masted schooner.

  "Never before had such wonderful bridging been attempted," wrote Nevin O. Winter in 1918. "Many said it was absolutely impossible. In one instance, at least, the distance is so great that the horizon closes in on the opposite terminus. In the construction it was necessary to build towers for sighting the instruments, for the curvature of the earth rendered the rodman on the key undistinguishable from the man with transit."

Interestingly, the idea of a railroad to Key West from the mainland was first put forth at the dawn of America's railway era in 1831 by the editor of the *Key West Gazette*. Several plans were hatched through the 1800s, mainly because Key West was Florida's most populous city from around 1840 to 1890. How could the southeast's deepest shipping port—the "American Gibraltar," as one congressman put it—remain isolated from the rest of Florida? When Henry Flagler helped put Miami on the map by extending the Florida East Coast Railway to the city in 1896, the vision of a Keys railroad came into clearer focus. Engineering surveys began in 1902, and the project gained steam when the federal government decided to build the Panama Canal, giving the Key West port even more prominence.

Henry Flagler was 75 years old when he gave his vice president, Joseph Parrott, the green light: "…go ahead. Go to Key West." Perhaps we can understand Flagler's motivation a bit by this 1906 statement: "I have always been contented, but I have never been satisfied."

A few folks paddled between the old and new bridges of the seven-mile crossing while others stopped at Molasses Key, an overnight stop along the 1,515-mile Florida Circumnavigational Saltwater Paddling Trail around the entire state. Lunch was on another uninhabited island, Money Key, as idyllic an island as you could ask for with a sandy beach and palms. Monica Woll of Florida Bay Outfitters in Key Largo then guided the rear contingent to other islands on the way to Bahia Honda

State Park, including Rachel Carson Key, named after the famous environmental scientist. It pays to take your time and paddle in the rear, and I labeled the sweep section of the trip "Margaritaville" to connote the laid-back mood.

Paddling along the old Seven Mile Bridge, a.k.a. Knight's Key Bridge, towards Pigeon Key.

Monica gave a fascinating talk that evening about the Flagler Railroad and the historic bridges we were paddling alongside. A railroad to Key West, once considered Flagler's Folly, was later viewed as a herculean engineering feat and labeled "the eighth wonder of the world." It wasn't economically successful, however, and it suffered a slow decline to bankruptcy. The Labor Day Hurricane of 1935, perhaps the strongest in contemporary Keys history, served as a final blow. But without Flagler showing the way—and leaving sturdy bridge spans from Key Largo to Key West—the Overseas Highway might never have been built. And today, bicyclists and hikers utilize some of the original railroad spans on the Florida Keys Overseas Heritage Trail, making it the most popular state-managed park and trail unit in the system, generating more than $91 million a year in direct economic impact, according to the Florida Park System in 2013. Kayakers, too, enjoy paddling along the artistic concrete bridge arches built by Flagler, and being on the water, they have a better view of the spans.

German cement was used for most undertakings below the high tide line, a high quality cement that has been unmatched, thus one reason most of the pilings remain solid. To create the pilings, workers built dams around each one to keep out sea water. The total project took years. Thousands of men from a variety of professions, including unskilled laborers from New York's "skid row," were recruited to work. They were housed on various islands and on boats, and dangers from hurricanes and topical storms were ever present. One boat containing about 150 men broke away from its moorings during a 1906 storm and 100 men were lost. Less dangerous, but a near constant torment, were the mosquitoes and sand fleas, and this was cited as a main reason men quit their jobs.

The hurricanes prompted Flagler to focus on sturdier, though more expensive, materials. Concrete arches were preferred in many places over wood and steel trestles since they were more permanent.

The railroad was completed on January 22, 1912. Frail and in poor health at age 83, Flagler rode in on a special train with various distinguished guests. Upon his arrival, he received a grand ovation and Key West declared a three-day holiday. "Now I can die happy," Flagler told the throngs. "My dream is fulfilled." He died the next year.

Flagler biographer Edward Akin contends that Flagler built the Key West Extension not to enhance his personal wealth or position, but as an enduring monument. "There was no way an aging man would reap a profit from the venture," Akin wrote. "One must view the Key West Extension simply as Henry Flagler's gift to Florida—and his desire to be immortalized." Ironically, Flagler's rail bed and bridges are much more successful today as a non-motorized trail than they were when trains chugged to and from Key West.

Our camp at Bahia Honda State Park below the old Bahia Honda Rail Bridge.

A day off at Bahia Honda State Park was one of our trip's highlights. There was no better place to hike trails canopied by sea grape trees, savor ice-cream cones, join other paddlers in yoga on the abandoned bridge overlooking Bahia Honda Sound, and take a snorkeling trip on Looe Key Reef. I also got to try a sailing kayak under the tutelage of Jon Sairs of Vermont. Jon, his wife Ann, and his mother Sally, sailed their rigs for much of the trip since the winds were favorable. Jon is a dealer for the rigs. Such a peaceful and quiet way to move on the water.

We kayak-surfed the next day. Paddling 18 miles with a 10 to 15 mile-per-hour tailwind means riding waves most of the way to the Sugarloaf Key KOA. The only tricky part was in places where strong currents running under bridges would hit us broadside, prompting more rocking from side to side. I had placed some extra weight in the stern of my boat and that helped. Lunch was at the scenic Big Munson Island, managed by the Boy Scouts, where picnic tables are nestled in small tree-covered coves. Shade is always welcome during open water paddles.

The Sugarloaf Key KOA is one of the oldest campgrounds in the Keys and busy, with a large RV presence, but it also has a spacious tent camping area. Entertainment was provided by Tammerlin—Lee Hunter and Arvid Smith. The skilled duo hails from Jacksonville. "We're looking for any excuse to come down to the Keys," Lee said. We were a tough audience, however, because most people started yawning soon after dinner. It wasn't the music, just the sun, wind and exercise.

An unusual calm greeted us as we paddled out of Sugarloaf. Even the kayak sailing folks had to paddle. But once we rounded the point of Sugarloaf Key and headed in a westerly direction, our friend the tailwind greeted us ever so gently. Several in the group vowed to make it a leisurely paddle since this was our last full day—20 miles.

In one section, along an unspoiled mangrove shore of the Western Sambos Ecological Reserve, scores of brown pelicans dove for fish, ospreys circled, and white ibis probed the shallows. A manta ray shot out from beneath my boat, and a small shark worked the shoreline. This wildlife haven was a welcome treat.

Speaking of wildlife, our overnight stop at Boyd's Campground was fun with lots of spirits and snacks and a lively concert by Rod MacDonald. He was joined by Tammerlin for a few songs and most of us managed to stay awake for both entertaining sets. It was a fun way to spend our last evening together. The only drawback was the talkative and frisky young people in the campsite next to mine, making it difficult to sleep.

We paddled into Key West under clear skies and, you guessed it, with a strong tailwind! A gargantuan Disney cruise ship passed before us as we pulled into Fort Taylor State Park around the same time Henry Flagler first arrived on his Key West Extension a century ago. Everyone felt a sense of accomplishment. Flagler had enormous challenges in completing his dream and we had a few of our own, though not nearly as severe. Having a tailwind certainly helped.

As I closed my eyes that night, I could easily visualize the warm faces of my paddling companions and feel the gentle rocking of Atlantic waters along the Florida

Keys. The trip would soon become a memory, one cherished by those who participated.

Besides commemorating the Flagler centennial, the Keys Challenge was noteworthy for other reasons. At 11 days, it was the longest trip in terms of time that Paddle Florida has ever organized and it couldn't have happened without the flexibility and assistance offered by the Florida Park Service. If you've ever tried to get a reservation for a winter campsite in the Keys, you know how difficult it is, but try organizing camping for 70 people! Four state parks were utilized for camping—Pennekamp, Long Key, Curry Hammock and Bahia Honda. Fort Taylor State Park served as a fitting end point for the trip. Also, four private campgrounds were used along with a Boy Scout camp.

The Keys challenge was also the largest group to have ever paddled together from Key Largo to Key West in contemporary history and the largest group to have paddled a complete segment of the 1,515-mile Florida Circumnavigational Saltwater Paddling Trail. The feat will likely remain a benchmark for years to come.

If You Go

The Florida Keys have been a popular kayaking destination for years, and why not? The waters are often gin-clear, sea life is abundant, and there are coral reefs and numerous local and state parks along with bars and restaurants accessible from the water. Besides campgrounds, "mom and pop" motels are numerous. There are drawbacks, too. During the peak season in late winter and early spring, reservations are a must at all campgrounds and motels, and prices climb the closer to

Key West. Some private campsites can cost more than a motel room in other parts of the state.

    Segment 15 of the Florida Circumnavigational Saltwater Paddling Trail includes maps and guides for paddling the length of the Keys, http://www.dep.state.fl.us/gwt/paddling/Segments/Segment15/Segment%2015.htm. Also, a number of shorter paddling adventures are available. To learn more, check out *The Florida Keys Paddling Atlas* by Bill and Mary Burnham (Falcon Press), *The Florida Keys Paddling Guide* by Bill Keogh (Backcountry Press), *Kayaking the Keys* by Kathleen Patton (University Press of Florida), and other guides. Up-to-date trail information can be obtained by calling or visiting Florida Bay Outfitters in Key Largo (305) 451-3018 and other outfitters. Seeing the Keys by kayak is unlike any other experience in the United States, although open water stretches are recommended for experienced sea kayakers with proper equipment.

2
Peace among Mangroves at Weedon Island

Tampa Bay is home to one of Florida's busiest ports, complete with tanker ships, tugboats and industrial loading facilities, and Pinellas and Hillsborough counties are some of the most densely populated in the state with more than two million souls between them. And yet, amidst the congestion, or perhaps because of it, there are places like the Weedon Island Preserve, 3,700 acres of natural Florida.

Even before the first Spaniards, the place was special. Native Americans created a large shell mound and burial mound complex on the site, and the large village of Yat Kitischee was located five miles northwest. In the 1920s, part of the burial mound was excavated by J.

Walter Fewkes of the Smithsonian Institution, whereupon he uncovered ornate mortuary vessels archeologists came to associate with the Weeden (alternate spelling) Island Culture. The site is still regarded with reverence by contemporary Seminoles, a people largely descended from Creek peoples from Alabama and Georgia, but also from surviving members of early Florida tribes who withstood centuries of war, persecution and European-introduced diseases.

In 2011, a nearly 40-foot pine dugout canoe was excavated along the shoreline, far longer than any previously found in Florida, perhaps because it was directly associated with a saltwater environment. Carbon dating puts it anywhere from AD 690 to 1010.

The preserve itself was named after an early owner and amateur archaeologist, Dr. Leslie Weedon. He was the son of Frederick Weedon, the doctor who attended to Osceola after his capture and decided to lop off the famous war leader's head after he died. Frederick Weedon, a believer in phrenology—the study of skulls to determine mental abilities and character traits and now largely discredited—was said to have scared his kids with the skull if they misbehaved. No wonder Leslie Weedon sought refuge on a remote island along Tampa Bay, then only accessible by boat. And what of Osceola's skull? It was eventually destroyed by a fire.

Leslie Weedon hoped the island he came to love would become a preserve, but it took 37 years after his death in 1937 for his dream to become a reality. Pinellas County's Department of Environmental Management now manages the preserve along with other preserves and management areas totaling more than 11,000 acres.

So, what does all this have to do with outdoor adventure? Well, hearkening back to its early inhabitants, the Weedon Island Preserve has some of the most intriguing paddling in the region with more than four miles of marked trails through mangroves forests and isolated bays. My kayaking guide was an old friend, Safety Harbor resident Hank Brooks. Hank is past president of the Tampa Bay Sea Kayakers and the Florida Paddling Trails Association. He often volunteers to lead trips through the preserve along with other locations in the region such as the mangrove trails of Caladesi Island, Cockroach Bay on the south side of Tampa Bay, the paddle to and from Anclote Key, around Safety Harbor, and several sections of the Hillsborough River, including the lower stretch through downtown Tampa. So, there are plenty of area trails to keep one occupied.

Once we embarked from the Weedon Island launch site and entered the first mangrove tunnel, I realized it would be easy to get turned around if not for Hank's guidance and 38 signs that mark the four-mile trail. Only a few Florida paddling trails and trail systems are marked by signs, the most notable being the 190-mile Calusa Blueway system in Lee County. I was glad I brought my 14-foot craft because Hank had some difficulty making sharp turns in the tunnels in his 16.5-foot sea kayak. And a couple of the tunnels were so narrow that we had to break apart our paddles and use one end to paddle canoe style. Otherwise, the long two-ended paddle would have easily gotten hung up in the branches. A small canoe paddle would have worked nicely in these narrow stretches.

We paddled quickly, mainly because Hank was worried we might become stranded on a mud flat. "That's why we got started by eight o'clock," he said. "If we started an hour later, we wouldn't make it."

Low tide was set for noon and water was rushing out of the mangroves and bays. Water depth was only six inches in many places. A rising tide would have allowed for a more leisurely, stress-free paddle, but I had to head home in the afternoon.

We passed beneath stretches of boardwalk that mark some of the preserve's nearly five miles of walking trails, and we crossed the shadow of a three-story viewing tower. "The county [Pinellas] set up many of these parks when they had money," Hank said. "Now that they've had to cut budgets, they've cut staff and they're struggling to maintain what they have."

Weedon Island Preserve from wildlife tower.

The mangrove openings were havens for birds—great blue herons and reddish egrets, tri-colored herons and the curve-billed white ibis. Ospreys called and some soared past clutching fish. Breakfast!

The contrasts of paddling the Weedon Preserve are interesting. For much of the time, you are enclosed in great leafy corridors, bordered by mangrove prop roots that make the trees appear to the walking a la *Lord of the Rings* style. Then you pop out into small bays that open up into the broader Tampa Bay, providing hazy views of multi-story buildings in Tampa and St. Petersburg, smokestacks of power plants, and huge loading docks and giant vessels. You can imagine an early Indian glimpsing the future, and not wanting to believe what would befall his beloved bay. At least an active group of individuals had the foresight to create this reservation for native plants and animals and for the well-being of human visitors. Perhaps we can build smarter along the coast, mindful of the increasing severity of storms and ever rising sea levels. And more shorelines can revert back to mangroves and other natural buffers that resemble the incredible Weedon Island Preserve.

If You Go

Pinellas County's Weedon Island Preserve is the perfect melding of cultural and natural preservation. It is open daily from 7 a.m. to just before sunset, although the visitor's center is open Thursday through Saturday from 9 to 4. From the west side of the Gandy Bridge over Tampa Bay, proceed west on Gandy Boulevard to San Martin Boulevard and turn south. Travel one mile and turn east onto Weedon Drive NE and you will reach the preserve's main gate. For more information, log onto http://www.weedonislandpreserve.org/.

3
Titusville's Magical Glowing Waters

"...It is not the property of fire alone to give light;...small drops of the water, struck off by the motion of the oars in rowing, seem sparkling and luminous."
    Francis Bacon, 1605

"I often see hogs and deer on this road," author Susan Young was saying as we drove after dark towards the Haulover Canal in the Merritt Island National Wildlife Refuge near Titusville. "Not too long ago, I accidently hit two wild hogs not too far from here."

Thus the reason we were creeping along at school-zone speed, headlights peering into a moonless night.

Just then, a five-foot alligator jumped onto the road. "Whoa!" Susan and I shouted simultaneously as she expertly swerved, barely missing the gleaming reptile. She exhaled loudly. "That's why I'm driving so slow!"

We were part of a group with the Florida Outdoor Writers Association taking a late night adventure with A Day Away Kayak Tours to experience the watery bioluminescence that has made the region famous. The best time to see the glowing dinoflagellates is from mid-July to mid-September when the waters are warmest, and since we were visiting at the tail end of the season, the unique happening would likely be weaker. But, as evidenced by the suicidal alligator, lots of others critters were still active on this night.

Upon arriving at the Haulover Canal—originally a place where people dragged boats overland between the Mosquito Lagoon and Indian River Lagoon before a canal was dug—I quickly ascertained the booming popularity of the bioluminescence tours. About thirty people in a high school group were just finishing their tour while another large group was embarking. Floodlights beamed down on an area around a small trailer and beach where the tour company was situated. Smaller tour companies were set up nearby. They also had skin in this dinoflagellate game. Altogether, the unique eco-tourism enterprises have helped to ease the regional impact of budgetary reductions in the space program. And while bioluminescence occurs in other Florida waters, the Titusville region has been the primary one to capitalize on it.

Our group of fifteen signed waivers and picked up our gear, gear that included green glow sticks that we hung off our backs so people behind us could follow. We were soon paddling across a bay of unknown distance, following a leader whose blinking red light guided the way, like Rudolph. We could see dark silhouettes of other paddling groups on the water, their undulating lines of green glow sticks moving serpent-like through the night. Somewhere in the blackness, leaping mullet occasionally slapped the surface.

The wind was up so it was difficult to see the tiny bioluminescent single cell dinoflagellates until we entered a quiet cove. Then, each dip of the paddle created a starlit effect of soft green flashes, reminding me of electrical sparks.

The water only glowed when we paddled—cause and effect. That's because dinoflagellates emit their light when disturbed, and if that disturbance has been caused by a would-be predator, that predator might reconsider. Scientists believe that the brief flash is meant to attract a secondary predator that could prey upon the initial predator, thus making the initial predator less likely to mess with these troublesome lightning bugs of the sea.

Most dinoflagellates are microscopic, although the largest variety is two millimeters in diameter. And about ninety percent are considered to be marine plankton. Chlorophyll is key to the efficient chemical reactions that excite electrons and produce no heat. The brightness of the night-time flashes directly correlates to the intensity of the previous day's sunlight.

Dinoflagellates aren't the only sea creatures that emit light. A whopping ninety percent of marine organisms are believed to have the capability of producing light, but often for different reasons. Some, such as the angler fish, use bioluminescence to attract prey, while others use it to communicate to others of their kind or to better see in deep ocean voids.

Along the edge of the mangroves, we stirred up oval comb jellies that emitted longer flashes of soft green light. They resembled glowing eggs bumping around the mangrove prop roots. And invisible mosquitoes realized an opportunity. The nuisance of swarming swamp angels was well worth it, however, for this was a unique opportunity. "It's just neat paddling at night like this," Susan said.

"Yeah," I agreed, "but I mostly paddle under the full moon. This is totally different."

We listened for, but did not hear, the periodic thumping mating calls of black drum beneath the surface, a sound known to even penetrate sea walls in South Florida. Nor did we startle a manatee, dolphin or large alligator, a much more common occurrence. Thousands of glowing tiny creatures were enough.

As we wound our way down the Haulover Canal, toward the glowing light of the launch area, the midnight hour was upon us. It would soon be time for us to turn off our lights and leave these quiet coves to the dinoflagellates and other creatures, the magic night soon to be a glowing memory.

If You Go

Bioluminescent kayak tours in the Titusville area are available in the summer months. For more information about A Day Away Kayak Tours, log onto http://www.adayawaykayaktours.com or call 321-268-2655. Tours start around sunset and last about two hours. Book ahead on weekends. Of course, you might discover other places around Florida where the water has bioluminescence. Get out on a warm dark night and find out!

4
On Being a Lunatic

The sinking sun glowed crimson as the rising full moon soon cast an ethereal light upon the water. Bats whisked in and out of shadows. Cormorants and wading birds quietly settled on tree branches for the night while hooting barred owls and bellowing frogs echoed from the growing darkness. Color faded as the world transformed into a black and white panorama.

It was the perfect time to begin our canoeing trip on the Wakulla River.

My companions in the canoe, David and Tom, alternated from silence to talking of the river and its creatures. No discussions of work or sports or wives. Just the river.

Fish splashed and popped. Leaping mullet slapped the water as they landed. Tom wished aloud for a fishing pole. Then a very large splash startled us, probably too big for a freshwater fish. Our theories as to what caused the splash ranged from an alligator to a manatee to a disoriented tarpon or inland shark.

One of the added elements of moonlight paddling is the unknown—being unable to see the source of various sounds and movements. The total effect of the moon can be mystifying. While paddling down the river, our main concern was the moon's influence on us. One minute we were loud, the next silent or, inexplicably, we found ourselves whispering. And then Tom had periodic impulses to play his banjo and bellow country tunes, even though he had only been playing for two months.

People once believed, and some still do, that if one falls under the spell of the full moon's unearthly light, he or she is a "lunatic," derived from the Latin word "luna," meaning moon. Many people today use this word in a different context and call people "loonies" for paddling down a river or across an open body of water at night. Little do they realize that being a "loony" is great fun, so long as a few precautions are taken before embarking.

We chose the spring-fed Wakulla south of Tallahassee because of its relatively wide flow, with no major side rivers or creeks branching from it. The river is also free of large snags and rapids, further reducing the risk of tipping over. And we checked the weather forecast beforehand, ensuring that it was a clear night with little chance of fog or high winds.

As we slowly rounded the river bends, each of us casting a different shadow upon the water, we were inclined to veer into the moonlit portion of the river. The watercourse was silver on black, a changing silhouette of trees against a luminescent sky. Indefatigable choruses emanated from unseen sloughs and clumps of water weeds. Some were identifiable, those of frogs and insects. Others were not. The noise lowered for a moment as if someone turned down the volume.

"You know, when I was a kid," I said, breaking the spell, "my grandmother used to be so afraid of snakes that she'd carry a big stick with her every night when she'd walk near the lake. And one night she nearly beat our neighbor's garden hose to death!"

The frogs, insects and other noisemakers began their cacophony once again, this time in an almost deafening crescendo. Tom broke in with a country tune. We laughed, telling him to shut up or else all of the night's creatures will be upon us. All the while, the white orb of the full moon followed our passage in the water.

We rounded a few more bends and the Highway 98 Bridge loomed ahead. We topped off our home-stretch with a few moonlight snacks. More fish jumped. Or could they be gators? We pull up to a glowing sand bank beside the bridge and began unloading the canoe. The river kept flowing, but the full moon reflecting on the water was now motionless, as if taunting us to go farther.

If You Go

In planning your trip, choose a clear, calm night with no threat of storms, high winds or dense fog. Look up the exact time for the moonrise in the newspaper, an almanac or online and make sure it is rising over the horizon by the time you embark. Otherwise, you may be in for an hour or more of darkness. Always bring a flashlight or headlamp, just in case.

Calm lakes and protected bays and estuaries work well for a moonlight trip. If choosing a river, select one with a wide flow, with no major side rivers or creeks branching from it. Scout it ahead of time during daylight. The river should also be free of snags or rapids, and the take out point should be easily spotted in low light conditions. If not dropping off a vehicle at a prearranged take out point, plan to paddle against the current first so you can float back during the second half of the trip when your arms might be getting tired. For information on the Wakulla River mentioned in the chapter, log onto http://www.dep.state.fl.us/gwt/guide/paddle.htm.

For spotting night creatures, a good flashlight or headlight works well. It is advisable to tie a piece of red cellophane over the beam in order not to blind owls and other night creatures with sensitive eyes. If paddling on southern rivers or lakes, scan the shore with a flashlight for red alligator eyes. The farther apart the eyes, the bigger the gator!

Other practical items are bug repellent and warm clothing for the cool night air. Ensure that everyone wears their life jackets since water rescues at night can be more challenging. If traveling on a water body that might have boat traffic, place a battery operated running light on your canoe or kayak bow and, if paddling in a group, stay close together. If nervous about moonlight paddling, check with local outfitters or paddling clubs. They often plan moonlight excursions.

In your preparations, don't forget the midnight snacks and drinks! Nothing is better than food in the great outdoors under a full moon. And remember to just have fun and let loose a little, maybe do a little howling. OwwwWoooo! That's what being a lunatic is all about.

5
When You Need a Guide: Paddling the Thousand Islands

Kayaking in unfamiliar territory can be tricky, especially in places such as the Thousand Islands near Cocoa Beach along Florida's East Coast. No, this isn't the Ten Thousand Islands along the southern edge of the Florida Peninsular, but you can get just as lost. And, it has a similar appearance, with mazes of tidal creeks and mangrove islands. That's why I jumped at the chance to paddle the Thousand Islands with Jim Durocher of Space Coast Kayaking in 2012.

We launched at a small landing at the Cocoa Beach Country Club, a misnomer since this was a public park. Jim initially led us on a broad waterway, but we soon ducked into a canopied mangrove tunnel where the real fun began. It was single file through here with sides lined with tall prop roots that are unique to red mangroves—like spiders frozen in place. Long seed pods dangled overhead, sometimes brushing our heads. Cries of osprey filled the air, and when we came to small openings, we watched them soaring overhead. There were no trail markers nor trail maps for this region, so a guide was essential. Plus, Jim provided some area history.

"During the Apollo space program, this area was booming and there were plans to build bridges to these islands and develop them, but those plans fell through when the Apollo program ended and the demand wasn't there," he said.

Enter Brevard County's Environmentally Endangered Lands program (EEL), created when a $55 million bond referendum was passed by Brevard County citizens in 1990. More than 13,000 acres were purchased, including the Thousand Islands. The area is now known as the Thousand Islands Conservation Area, frequented by paddlers, boaters and hikers. "This was the perfect storm where people, the environment, and the EEL program were all winners with the successful acquisition of the Thousand Islands," concluded state representative Tony Sasso when the last island was purchased.

Jim would like to see paddling trail maps and guides developed and a spur trail that branches from the 1515-mile Florida Circumnavigational Saltwater Paddling Trail around Florida's entire coast, but for now, we have people like Jim to serve as guides and I was glad we did.

Jim described the differences between red, white and black mangroves. He pointed out buttonwood bushes,

Jim Durocher describing the Thousand Islands area.

a favorite wood of pioneers for smoking mullet. He pointed out osprey, anhinga, dolphin and a couple of manatees. "The manatees sometimes congregate in here," he said. "But we've had a seagrass die-off due to algae blooms." Nonetheless, the Indian River Lagoon remains the most biologically diverse estuary in Florida, utilized by more than 2,200 species of animals and 2,100 varieties of plants, partly due to its unique position as an overlapping border for both tropical and subtropical species. It's like paddling through a zoo with no cages. And it helps to have a guide on this kayaking safari.

If You Go
  To book a Thousand Island tour with Space Coast Kayaking, log onto http://www.spacecoastkayaking.net .

or call 321-784-2452. For more information about the Thousand Islands region, log onto the website of the Friends of the Thousand Islands Sanctuary: http://www.friends1000islands.com/about-us.html.

6
The Wekiva Promise

The shuttle van wasn't banged up enough. At least, that was the observation of the guy next to me after we had crammed in 16 people for a ride to King's Landing along Rock Springs Run just north of Orlando. And this guy sounded as though he should know, having embarked on paddling trips throughout North America.

"These vans usually look like they've been to hell and back," he said, "with parts of the dash held together with duct tape. Except for that hole in the driver's side floor, this one looks to be in decent shape. I'm worried." Just then the driver hopped in, picked up a flathead screw driver, stuck it into the ignition and turned. The engine roared to life noisily and a dash light remained on. "Phew, now I feel better," the guy said. We determined that the hole in the driver's side floor was to help stop the van if necessary, a la Flintstones style.

On a crystalline fall day, temperatures rising into the 70s, our Paddle Florida group of fifty was soon floating down a spring-fed, sand-bottomed stream. Sabal palms arched over us. Bunches of purple asters lined the shores and brilliant red leaves of Florida maple reminded us of winter's approach and the fact that other parts of the country were already digging out of snowstorms. The closest thing to snow we encountered were fluffy white seeds that floated from tall Sea Myrtle (baccharis) shrubs along the shore. The red berries on dahoon holly trees, though, were a sure sign of the approaching Florida winter, along with clumps of round green mistletoe in the tops of near barren deciduous trees, reminiscent of Dr. Seuss illustrations.

Golden leaves rained down upon us in gentle breezes as we glided down the moving path. Fall is a time for reflection and I remembered the first time I visited Wekiwa Springs State Park. The year was 1976 and at age nineteen, I was attending an organizational meeting of the Friends of Florida State Parks at the same meeting hall where our Paddle Florida group heard talks about the Wekiva Basin the night before we embarked. That early meeting was facilitated by then chief state park naturalist Jim Stevenson. At some point, I naively asked Jim, "Do you have any plans to cut the trees around here?" Being new to the environmental movement, I had become painfully aware of how private timber companies and public land managers with the U.S. Forest Service were clearcutting vast swaths of increasingly rare upland longleaf pinewoods and other habitats.

Stevenson suppressed a smirk. "No, we hope these longleaf pines will be here long after I am gone," he said. I was just learning the basics of conservation. While state parks actively promote recreation, they also protect and restore native habitat, and Wekiwa Springs was doing a good job of restoring and managing its increasingly rare longleaf pine habitat with frequent prescribed burns.

For the next several years, I returned to Wekiwa Springs State Park for annual meetings of the Florida Sierra Club. While the park itself didn't change a great deal—except for rising visitation levels—roads leading to the park became increasingly congested as development pushed up against the park's boundaries. I came to understand how some parks can become islands of biodiversity, the need for good stewardship even more vital. Fortunately, county governments and the state have been able to purchase additional conservation lands to the east and north, establishing a protected black bear corridor all the way to the Ocala National Forest and to the Lake Woodruff National Wildlife Refuge. Bears are plentiful in the region, as evidenced by the large male that frequented our Paddle Florida camp at the park.

Paddling one of Florida's two federally designated wild and scenic rivers, it was difficult to fathom that more than two million people live within thirty miles of the Rock Springs Run/Wekiva River system. Water was sparkling clear, turtles sunned on logs, limpkins probed for apple snails in vast mats of native spadderdock and pennyroyal, and there was not a speck of invasive hydrilla to be found. "The Wekiva is considered one of the most protected waters in the state," Wekiva aquatic preserve manager Deborah Shelley told us before we embarked, "but we still have challenges in the basin."

Excess nutrients are the hidden menace. Fertilizers from lawns, golf courses and farms along with septic tank discharges and other sources have entered the groundwater and have emerged in springs that feed Rock Springs Run and the Wekiva River, so much so that reported nitrate concentrations have been 480 percent higher than the maximum levels for healthy waters. That's because vast tracts of public land that make up this watery wilderness do not encompass the entire recharge area. And so, solutions fall upon area residents and farmers.

A welcome champion—the Rotary Club of Seminole County South—recently put forth a challenge to area residents to reduce nutrient levels in the springs. Working with river managers and water and landscaping experts, they put together a glossy, magazine-style publication about the river basin's biodiversity and the need for protection measures. The culmination is a simple and straightforward promise that people can make:
--I will use less fertilizer, no fertilizer or slow-release fertilizer on my lawn.
--I will have my septic tank inspected and, if needed, pumped out every five years.
--I will plant native or drought tolerant trees, shrubs, and ground cover.
--I will use pesticides and herbicides only when absolutely necessary.
--I will write a letter to my local government official, county commissioner and/or state legislators to let them know I support protecting the Wekiva River Basin.

Perhaps because it is backed by science and is not the rant of perceived radical environmentalists, the promise is taking hold. "Governments alone cannot protect our water resources," concluded Rotary president Jim DeKleva.

Will clear results be realized? Time will tell, but the pledge is the main hope to reduce pollution short of stringent regulations and the expensive phasing out of septic tanks for more advanced treatment options. Water conservation, xeric landscaping and rainwater catchment should be additional pledge items since flows in the river system's main springs have been below established minimum flows and levels in 2011 and 2012, and they have steadily declined since the 1930s, correlating with human population explosions in the region.

Black-crowned night heron along the Wekiva River.

What is at stake in the basin is impressive—more than 120 species of birds, eight species of turtles, and numerous threatened and endangered plants and animals. And more species—and even new springs—are being discovered in the 300-square-mile basin. In April of 2012, Friends of the Wekiva River initiated a three-day "BioBlitz" in which more than 175 scientists, college students and naturalists participated in an extensive biological survey of the Wekiva basin. The results were astounding. Of the 1,564 species of animals and plants found, 36 percent of the total number of plant species—212—were previously undocumented. "This made it fun for all of our botanists while we were out there," exclaimed botany team leader Randy Mejeur after the event.

Young raccoon along the Rock Springs Run.

The mammal team leader, biologist Jack Stout, was surprised at finding a relative abundance of the Florida mouse, believed to be a rare species and only found in limited areas of Florida. "If this animal is doing well, the wilderness is happy," he said.

"We are in a biodiversity hotspot of global significance," concluded conservation biologist Reed Noss after the event when the results were tallied.

Ecologist Dr. Jay Exum added that the basin needs to remain "big, wild and connected" to ensure that its biodiversity is sustained.

And the lifeblood for much of the area's biodiversity is clean and abundant fresh water.

"It's natural to cheer the biological diversity of this singular river system—and to be thankful that 110 square miles of public land exists here," wrote author and environmental spokesman Bill Belleville in the *Orlando Sentinel* in 2013. "Yet, there's great irony at work: Just as we're unlocking the secrets about this rare landscape our elected officials are busy squandering the springs and the aquifer that fuels them. The fact they do so by ignoring its complex and finite limitations is not just obtuse, it's downright criminal. ... If any question needs a responsible answer, it is this: How much more potable water can we draw from our aquifer before the prehistoric seawater that comprises most of it begins to flow from our faucets?"

There are also human and economic factors involved in protecting and restoring the Wekiva basin. Wekiwa Springs State Park receives more than 250,000 visitors a year, and thousands more visit other parks and refuges in the region. And there are anglers like the one we met in a canoe along the river soon after embarking.

He lifted an impressive bass on a stringer. "There's some really big fish in this river," he said.

On our trip, as the waterway became more canopied, a mother raccoon along shore sounded an alarm. Four young raccoons scurried up a tree as the mother called from the ground. The young kept climbing to where they could barely cling to the uppermost branches and not fall. I backed away and watched as they climbed down safely to rejoin their mother. I wondered about the challenges of raising a raccoon brood along the Rock Springs Run/Wekiva River—alligators, bobcats, scary paddlers… Mammal mothers are worriers.

In places along the river, fern gardens are everywhere. And dancing in the current below us, we could see vast beds of eel grass and darting fish. Every bend is a pull on the senses to see, feel, hear and smell. Three planned days to paddle only 30 miles is fortuitous—there is no need to rush. The river beckons one to slow down. And other benefits can be realized. There is more time and energy in late afternoon to explore local human attractions.

After our second day, a group from Cincinnati gave a humorous report of one place they labeled "the tiki bar from *Deliverance*." To order a cheeseburger meant to be given a frozen patty, bun, and slice of American cheese and shown where the outside grill is located. If fortunate, a man will bring out diced onions and mustard in packets. And to root for an opposing football team while a game blasts on the bar's television is to incur the wrath of the female bartender who swats at customers with a kayak paddle and, if unsuccessful, she might throw an unopened can of beer. But it was all in good fun.

I had to leave the group on the last day as they embarked for the St. Johns River from Wilson's Landing Park. I was giving a talk that evening to the Tampa Bay Sea Kayakers. But on the advice of Jim Duby with Seminole County, I did have time to hike to the St. Johns River through the 1,650-acre Black Bear Wilderness Area, one of several large tracts protected by Seminole County as a result of a natural areas referendum passed by voters. The two- mile round-trip trail likely has the largest volume of bear scat—some very fresh—than any Florida footpath.

Just a few miles northwest was the Seminole State Forest. Probably some of the same bears that frequented the Bear Reserve had kept me up all night when I was the only one camping in the forest. They were all around my tent, walking heavy-footed while grunting and snorting. Morning found me sleeping uncomfortably curled up in the front seat of my car. The thin nylon of my tent just wasn't enough of a barrier. Fresh bear scat was all around my campsite. But that is a different story. I preferred to savor memories of a river that still flows wild under the Florida sun. Here's a shout out to those working to keep it that way.

If You Go

Emerging just north of Kelly Park in Apopka, Rock Springs Run winds through largely wild country for 7.5 miles until it joins the spring run flowing out of Wekiwa Springs State Park. From there, the river flows about 15 more miles to the St. Johns River. A good take-out spot is the High Banks Landing about two miles north along the St. Johns River on the eastern shore.

Both spellings, "Wekiva" and "Wekiwa," are used for various names in the area and most interpretive guides agree that they mean "spring of water" in the Muscogee language. Another interpretation has suggested that "Wekiva" means "flowing water" and "Wekiwa" means "bubbling water."

Four primitive state park campsites can be reserved along Rock Springs Run by calling 407-884-2008. Additionally, farther downstream, riverside primitive camping is available at the privately-operated Wekiva Falls RV Park, 407-830-9828.

For more information about the Wekiva River/Rock Springs Run Paddling Trail, log onto http://www.dep.state.fl.us/gwt/guide/designated_paddle/Wekiva_guide.pdf. Log on here for information about the Friends of the Wekiva River, http://www.friendsofwekiva.org/index.html.

7
Devilish Limpkins and Seminole Echoes on the Withlacoochee South

Withlacoochee—Little Great Water or Little River in the Muscogee/Seminole tongue

Limpkins. Happy limpkins! Before I joined Paddle Florida's first-ever Wild Wonderful Withlacoochee Adventure in February of 2013, I was aware of the region's history, how it was a stronghold for Seminole Indians early in the Second Seminole War, but I didn't know it was a modern-day limpkin haven. Around most bends, limpkins were probing, eating and calling. They have disappeared from other Florida rivers, but they are thriving along the Withlacoochee's middle section, possibly due to an invasion of non-native apple snails that have increased their food supply.

We began the five-day trip at Sumter County's Marsh Bend Outlet Park near Lake Panasoffkee. Sumter County officials, excited about the possibility of enhanced nature-based tourism in the area, had allowed us to camp in a spacious meadow beneath arms of live oaks—a first for the park—and now a campground was in the works thanks to Paddle Florida.

Morning sun tickled the water as we launched and made our way down the Outlet River to the wider Withlacoochee. Birds lined the shores—white ibis, herons, great and snowy egrets, and then there were the limpkins. In fact, I had never seen so many limpkins. Seminoles are gone from this place—driven south into the Everglades long ago or relocated west to present-day Oklahoma, but the birds have remained. Perhaps those early Seminoles would have been pleased about that. And now paddlers have returned to the river, too.

We were soon lowered about two feet through the lock at the Wysong Dam, a first for many. The dam was built to help keep water in the upper river. Paddlers can also portage around the dam at an airboat jump on the opposite side, being ever wary of approaching airboats. Fortunately, we would not see an airboat during the entire trip while paddling, perhaps due to the cool weather.

Clouds darkened by afternoon and a steady rain fell for the last two hours of paddling to Potts Preserve. Prior to the Withlacoochee, Paddle Florida had only one day of rain in 20 trips—over 100 days of paddling. As Paddle Florida executive director Bill Richards concluded, "We knew it wouldn't last forever." The forecast was for rain much of the night, so many of us took refuge at the nearby Turner's Fish Camp. They had a bar set up beneath a cozy

Seminole-built chickee and a warm fire in the rain. The fish camp owners were kind enough to allow us to have dinner under their pavilion and to listen to the lively musical duo of Tammerlin—Lee Hunter and Arvid Smith. The camp probably set a record for beer sales for a February weekday, especially a rainy one, thanks to Paddle Florida.

"You people are really interesting," exclaimed one of the gray-bearded fish camp regulars through a handful of teeth. "We hope you come back tomorrow night!" The cultural exchange did continue the next night—Old Florida meets active retirees. Only a handful in the Paddle Florida group still worked regular jobs.

A fun evening at the fish camp didn't guarantee good sleeping. One annoying trait of camping beside a river that has a high concentration of limpkins is the bird's screeching wake-up call in the wee hours. Roosters don't hold a candle to limpkins. The brown and white speckled birds are aptly named "the crying bird," and at four in the morning, they are the Devil's alarm clock. According to limpkin expert Dana Bryan, the offending limpkin was likely an unattached male seeking the company of a female since unattached females often fly along the river at night during mating season. Obviously, our single male limpkin didn't get lucky, and kept calling...and calling. Perhaps it's like crooning all night at a woman's window and the beautiful damsel never invites you in.

I wondered if Seminole warriors could imitate the limpkin's mournful cry. Osceola's war cry was said to have elicited spine-tingling chills. In fact, his name meant "Black Drink Singer," someone who plays an important part of the annual Green Corn Ceremony, so he must have had a voice for song, and war cries. Though not a designated chief, Osceola was in his prime during battles along the Withlacoochee and he became a respected war leader.

Several skirmishes were fought along the river, the first when General Duncan Clinch came to the river with 750 men on New Year's Eve in 1835 in an attempt to drive the Seminoles from the area. The ultimate goal was to remove the Indians from Florida to make room for white settlement, and to recapture escaped slaves. Clinch was unaware of what had befallen Major Francis Dade three days earlier, when Seminoles killed the major and more than a hundred of his men in a four-hour battle along the military road between Fort Brooke and Fort King—Florida's version of Custer at the Little Big Horn. The 100-mile road ran along the western boundary of the Seminole stronghold known as the Cove of the Withlacoochee. The Cove, now called Lake Tsala Apopka, consists of thick hammocks, swamps and a string of lakes, islands and peninsulas. The Withlacoochee River arches around the cove's eastern and northern borders, flowing north, not south.

Clinch, like most American generals, believed the Seminoles were divided by infighting, unable to muster a large capable fighting force. At a deep, swift point along the river, he and his men found a leaky dugout and began crossing seven and eight men at a time. The Seminoles, thinking Clinch would cross at a shallow ford a few miles downstream, quickly moved upstream by land to set up an ambush.

Clinch's regulars crossed first—about 250 in all—leaving a few hundred Florida Militia members along the western shore, their tours of duty set to expire the next day. The regulars moved about 150 yards inland to a clearing surrounded by a dense hammock and took a rest break. John Bemrose, an enlisted soldier in the outfit, described what happened next: "An officer, Capt. [Charles] Mellon, was the first to discern an Indian skulking in the thicket and having obtained permission of his battalion colonel to fire, which he had not sooner done than it was answered by the peeling sound of 1000 rifles fired amidst the troops simultaneously, followed by the unearthly war whoop from a thousand savage throats. The suddenness of the thing, conjoined to the terrible and bloodcurdling cry of the Indians, struck at once terror and some degree of panic among the soldiers, and they retreated precipitously to where the surgeons were placed, leaving about 20 of their comrades weltering in their blood." Several officers were quickly shot—a Seminole tactic—increasing the level of confusion.

  The one-armed Colonel Alexander Fanning appealed to Clinch for permission to charge the hammock with bayonets. Clinch turned him down twice, but, as described by Bemrose, Fanning made a third appeal, tears in his eyes: "General, my men will all be cut down. Oh, let me charge and my life for it, they will run!" The subsequent charge, and two others, may have saved Clinch's force from annihilation and allowed the force to retreat to the river. A makeshift bridge was created and the regulars moved to the northern shore, carrying 59 wounded with them. Four had lost their lives. The death toll would have been higher had the Seminoles used larger bore rifles. Seminole leaders claimed their casualties were three killed and five wounded.

Clinch retreated north to Fort Drane, realizing the Seminoles would not be easily uprooted from the Cove. Osceola sent a chilling letter to Clinch: "You have guns and so have we... You have powder and lead, and so have we... Your men will fight, and so will ours, till the last drop of Seminole's blood has moistened the dust of his hunting ground."

Ironically, Clinch was later called "Old Withlacoochee" in a run for Georgia governor, having somehow turned his retreat into victory in a way only skilled politicians can accomplish.

The Cove came under attack again that February when General Edmund Gaines and nearly one thousand men—with scant rations—repeatedly attempted to cross the Withlacoochee to round up the Seminoles. Seminole snipers repelled the troops and Gaines retreated to the northern shore, but instead of leaving the area like Clinch, Gaines built a log fortification he named Camp Izard, in honor of a fallen soldier. His plan was to draw in the entire Seminole fighting force of about 1,100 warriors so that when Clinch arrived with reinforcements, they could finish them off. The first part of Gaines' plan worked perfectly—he was soon surrounded on three sides. But where was Clinch?

At one point, black and Indian warriors started a brush fire that raced down towards the fortress. They attacked from behind the smoke screen. Abruptly, the wind shifted; fire swept back on the warriors. They hastily retreated. A long siege ensued.

Lieutenant Henry Prince described one skirmish in his diary that revealed the weakness of their breastworks: "Whang! Whang! Pop! Fit! Whirr! Bang! Spatter spatter

spatter! ... I ran to my line company amidst a storm of bullets. The Indians were round us as represented by the dots. There were at least 1000. They kept at a long distance. The fight was a very smart one for 3 hours. ... It seems to me impossible for bullets to fly thicker anywhere then they did round me. They would cut holes through the palmetto leaves 3 feet from us while others would fall dead all round me. I was hit by two spent balls one in the hip and one in the back." One rifle ball knocked out two of General Gaines' teeth. The soldiers built the breastworks higher.

    Days passed. Gaines sent desperate appeals to Clinch at Fort Drane, but Clinch was torn between conflicting orders from Gaines—commander of the western forces—and General Winfield Scott—commander of the eastern forces. Gaines ordered him to march immediately to his position along the Withlacoochee while Scott ordered him to stay. By courier, Clinch pleaded with Scott to reconsider—he could hear Gaines' distant cannons—but before receiving his reply, an impatient Clinch left with 500 men to rescue Gaines.

    With scant supplies and Seminole snipers picking off soldiers who ventured outside the log walls, Gaines' men were becoming weak, trying to live on small rations of butchered horses, mules and dogs. Some Seminoles, sensing an opportunity, called for a parley. Not all Seminoles were in agreement with this move, initiated by the black Seminole John Caesar, but Osceola stood by him. Negotiations began and Gaines seemed agreeable to recommend that all Seminoles be left alone south and west of the Withlacoochee, although he knew it was unlikely President Andrew Jackson would ever abide by such an agreement. The talks were cut short by the arrival of Clinch's troops, who immediately fired upon the Seminoles.

It was difficult to visualize the soldiers leaving the cramped enclosure after eight days. Many staggered. Some had to be carried. A few yelled and screamed as if they had gone mad. Several ate food so quickly they became violently ill.

By comparison, the scene at our Potts Preserve camp the morning after a rainy beer-soaked night at the fish camp and unwelcome limpkin wake-up calls was only mildly unpleasant. Still, we were a soggy looking bunch. And I noticed Advil bottles being pried open. Morning sun quickly lifted our spirits, however.

History buff Lars Anderson, also an author and kayak guide, led us four miles up the pristine Gum Slough in the morning. A perfect day—sunshine, adventure, and swimming in the headsprings! We had fun negotiating an obstacle course of rocks and logs, but we only had to step out of our boats once to portage.

Along the shore, blooming red cardinal flowers, yellow bur marigolds and blue flag irises added splashes of color to the emerging bright greens of budding leaves. There were flocks of white ibis and, of course, limpkins. Lars said the invasive apple snails had not made their way up Gum Slough and neither did we see any invasive hydrilla. The slough is largely protected by the 9,480-acre Half Moon-Gum Slough tract managed by the water management district, and the private landowner at the head springs has signed a conservation easement, ensuring that their property will not be developed beyond their personal dwellings.

Anderson, author of an excellent book about Paynes Prairie, is knowledgeable of the area's extensive history. Besides the Seminole war battles, Hernando De Soto tromped through in 1539 in search of adventure and gold. Spanish chain mail was found in a nearby shell mound along the river. A branch of the Timucuan tribe lived here for millennia until war and European introduced disease took their tolls.

Back on the Withlacoochee for day three, we spotted the largest cluster of feeding wading birds I've ever witnessed—about 30 great egrets and 75 white ibis. We also passed centuries old bald cypress trees. They were hollow, yet living, thus the reason early loggers spared them. They once towered over both Timucuan and Seminole Indians paddling the river. Living history landmarks.

Lunch was at Grey Eagle Park in the Stokes Ferry area, just upstream from the site of Camp Izard, where Seminoles laid siege to General Gaines and his men. The Seminole Wars Foundation, Inc., seeks to turn the unmarked battle site into a park with a museum and educational center since it is on undeveloped public land.

Camping at Rainbow Springs that evening, Dr. Bob Knight, founder of the Florida Springs Institute, gave us a sobering assessment of the state of Florida's incredible springs. His talk was a call to action on a freezing night. The evening before, we heard from David Rathke, chief-of-staff with the Southwest Florida Water Management District, about the district's efforts to address water problems. As people have poured into Florida, water quality and quantity has suffered. Only concerted efforts by both government and residents will solve the problems.

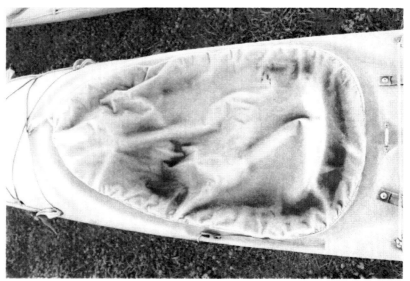
Frosty hatch cover on last morning of trip.

On a crisp morning, the upper Rainbow River was a sparkling kaleidoscope of emerald green eelgrass. Wood ducks, anhinga, heron and ibis were all warming in branches, and river otters—with their insulated fur—were swimming the river. With its high nitrate content, it is amazing the upper Rainbow is so clear. Dr. Knight says it is due to elevated dissolved oxygen content in the water, and, true to his observation, the eelgrass began to disappear farther downstream. By the time the river met the Withlacoochee, mats of filamentous algae—the curse of many Florida springs—covered the bottom.

We soon entered the wide marshy reaches of Lake Rousseau, being ever wary of stumps. Swallows, eagles and ospreys filled the skies, and countless American coots floated on the water's surface. Numerous wading birds poked along grassy islands. Even a handful of royal terns were perched on logs. A glorious day for birds and paddlers!

Lake Rousseau is one of Florida's oldest impounded lakes, dammed by the U.S. Department of Army in 1909. A few years ago, 1,800 stumps were removed from the marked boating channels, but the lake's backwaters have ample long-lasting cypress stumps and wetland areas. Motorboat traffic is rare outside of the marked channels, so it is a bird and paddler paradise. In one rookery area in the lake, 5,132 wading birds were counted around sunset. As with most rookeries, alligators help protect nesting birds from predators such as raccoons. Besides occasional disturbance by airboats and helicopters, the greatest threat to rookeries are significant water withdraws for human use.

Our camp was at the Inglis Lock where we heard a fascinating talk about the infamous Cross Florida Barge Canal by trail manager Mickey Thomason. Thomason manages the Cross Florida Greenway, a system of trails on land once slated for the canal. The dream of a canal bisecting Florida goes back to King Philip II of Spain in 1567. Rounding Florida was treacherous for his gold-bearing ships as evidenced by the numerous shipwrecks along the east coast and in the Keys. United States Secretary of War John C. Calhoun revived the idea in 1818, again citing shipwrecks and also piracy, but the first dirt wasn't turned until the Great Depression when a sea level canal was proposed, meaning that digging would need to go down more than 150 feet in central parts of the state. The project was cancelled in 1942 over concerns about aquifer damage, but it was revived again in the 1960s with a design for several locks and dams. After parts of the lower Withlacoochee and Ocklawaha Rivers were altered by canal construction, the project was halted by President Richard Nixon in 1971 as the nation's—and Florida's—environmental movement was gaining momentum and public support.

Today, the former canal lands are managed by the Florida Park Service. In a fitting tribute, the Cross Florida Greenway was named after the canal's chief opponent, Marjorie Harris Carr, while a dam on the lower Ocklawaha bears the name of a major canal proponent, former state senator George Kirkpatrick. I knew both in my early days of environmental lobbying. Carr was a raspy-voiced activisit and skillful organizer, while Kirkpatrick had a sense of bravado as evidenced by a large six-gun carrying poster of John Wayne that greeted visitors in his Senate office. Today, the canal dream is dead while more than 110 miles of hiking, biking and multi-use trails are managed by the greenway. A debate is still raging concerning the fate of the Kirkpatrick Dam and Rodman Reservoir along the lower Ocklawaha while the much older Lake Rousseau Reservoir is less controversial, perhaps due to the large numbers of bird rookeries in the lake.

When I opened my tent zipper for a call of nature in the morning, I was showered with frost. My kayak sponge was frozen solid. Even in central Florida, February camping can be unpredictable, and we had likely experienced winter's coldest night. Maybe a little hardship is appropriate along a river where so many fought and died. The war cries and cannon have long been silent, but the results of the Withlacoochee battles and those that followed helped to shape Florida's future along with the Seminole Nation.

The Seminoles, like nearly all of America's native peoples, stood in the way of Manifest Destiny. Ultimately, the Cove of the Withlacoochee wasn't large enough to conceal them. Only the vast swamps of the Everglades and Big Cypress successfully shielded a few remnant Seminole bands and allowed them to remain in this land they called home.

Slowly thawing, we paddled through the towns of Inglis and Yankeetown, passing numerous shrimp boats and other ocean-going vessels. Mullet leaped and coastal cedars and palms were numerous. Sun felt warm on my face—the previous night's freeze almost forgotten—and the Seminole battle sites and limpkins were many miles upstream. The historic Withlacoochee River was emptying into the Gulf as it always had, and I felt freer for gliding along with her.

If You Go

The 76-mile Withlacoochee River South Paddling Trail is ideal for a multi-day trip, or it can be divided into several day trips. There are some primitive campsites on public lands and a few fish camps and landings allow camping. A complete trail guide and maps can be accessed from the Florida Office of Greenways and Trails website: http://www.dep.state.fl.us/gwt/guide/designated_paddle/WithSouth_guide.pdf.

Low water levels can make paddling problematic in the upper half of the river, so check the online USGS gauge at Nobleton: http://waterdata.usgs.gov/fl/nwis/uv/?site_no=02312558&PARAmeter_cd=00065,00060. Water levels should be above 38.10 feet for ideal conditions.

8
Fishy Business on the Econlockhatchee

The Econlockhatchee River, Econ for short, is a blackwater river flowing through largely undeveloped lands just east of Orlando. The designated paddling trail begins at Highway 419, flows eight miles to the Little Big Econ State Forest Headquarters, and then another 11 miles to the State Road 46 Bridge. Many of the banks are tall and handsome, arching live oaks and palms form a shaded canopy in places, and numerous wading birds and alligators grace the shorelines. What more can you ask from a wild river? The problem during my mid-July paddling trip was dead fish and lots of them, and all catfish. That was a mystery. When you stepped in and out of the water, the slimy residue of dead fish covered feet and ankles.

I knew that two primary culprits cause most fish kills: blue-green algae blooms and low dissolved oxygen. Fish need to "breathe" just as land animals, but instead of using lungs, they absorb oxygen gases (dissolved oxygen) in the water through their gills.

Harmful algae blooms can be caused by warm weather combined with runoff and discharges from septic tanks, human development, farms, and other land-use activities that raises nitrogen and phosphorous levels in the water. Large algae blooms can block sunlight, often killing rooted water plants that are valuable fish habitat and reducing oxygen levels in the water. Some forms of the algae can be toxic to humans as well as to fish.

Low levels of dissolved oxygen in water can also be caused by high temperatures and low water levels because hot water holds less oxygen than cold water. Even extended periods of cloudy weather and high rainfall can cause fish kills because without the sun helping to produce oxygen, the system uses it up faster than it is produced. Plus, rainfall can flush organic materials such as grass clippings and leaves into the water and when these decompose, more oxygen is used.

So, some fish kills can occur due to both human related activities and natural weather patterns, or a combination of both. But what about the Econ River fish kill? To find the answers, I called the Florida Fish and Wildlife Commission Fish Kill hotline: 800-636-0511. A young man answered immediately and when I reported the problem, he said that several rivers and lakes in the St. Johns River watershed had experienced catfish kills since the end of May. Since water testing of the Econ River did not come up with any blue-green algae, the spokesman said that the kill was likely due to stress from spawning. Catfish congregate together in early summer to spawn and the process weakens their immune system. And because they are in close proximity during this time, they often scrape and cut each other with their spines, producing infections. "Most of the dead ones you saw probably died last week or before," he said. "It will likely start to clear up soon."

The explanation sounded a bit fishy to me. These catfish must be employing Klingon warrior type mating rituals (a la Star Trek) to produce so many injuries and deaths, so I asked my biologist friend Chad Hanson since he specializes in fishery issues. "I can't say he [FWC spokesman] isn't correct, but I've never heard of that and can't really find any other evidence of such an occurrence in a quick web search," he said. "Catfish are somewhat susceptible to low DO [dissolved oxygen], and since they are bottom dwellers where low DO typically occurs, that is the most plausible culprit. Plus, biologically speaking, it's not very good evolutionary strategy to form spawning aggregations that end up with self-induced mass die offs. Unless the population has gotten so big that that is a natural consequence somehow."

Evidently, catfish die-offs have occurred during other years at roughly the same time of year. So whatever the cause, I found that upon leaving the Econlockhatchee River, I needed to soak my ankles and water shoes in a vinegar solution to remove the dead fish smell, and only after a four-hour drive home!

If You Go

The 19-mile Econ River Paddling Trail can easily be divided into two day trips or a long day trip or an overnight trip. There are two primitive camping zones along the river in the Little Big Econ State Forest. For more information, log onto http://www.dep.state.fl.us/gwt/guide/designated_paddle/Econlock_guide.pdf. You just might want to avoid mid-summer.

9
The Santa Fe's Naked Man

Naked Ed. One of the last of Florida's colorful hermits. Talking with—not necessarily seeing—the famous nudist was one motivation to paddle North Florida's Santa Fe River in late February, rain or no rain. I had paddled the river a couple of years before, but Naked Ed was gone. He must have trekked into High Springs for supplies. Would he be there on a cold, rainy day?

    My two companions, Matt and Deb, were veteran paddlers. Deb had done long-distance trips in the Boundary Waters and Everglades while Matt was the first to paddle the 1,515-mile Florida Circumnavigational Saltwater Paddling Trail. A little rain was nothing more than a few gnats at sunset.

    Our plan was to launch at Rum Island County Park and paddle upstream to the Highway 27 Bridge and back for a total of eight miles. Several springs were located along the way, including Lily Spring where Naked Ed lived in a small hut.

    As we launched, the rain slowed to a drizzle, and once on the water, it stopped altogether. A swirling mist rose up from the water. As we easily paddled upstream, we passed a myriad of plate-sized turtles poking their heads above the surface. Numerous birds lined the shores or darted across our bows—great egrets, wood ducks, wood storks, white ibis, anhingas, bald eagles, buffleheads, great blue herons, crows, red-shouldered hawks, pileated woodpeckers and kingfishers. Most were in pairs and seemed unafraid. "It's like Noah's Ark," Matt observed. Indeed, if Noah had needed a near complete representation of North Florida riverine wildlife species, he would have come to the Santa Fe River. But would there have been any room for hermits in his survivalist scheme?

Deb Akin at Rum Island Spring along the Santa Fe.

A highlight was a pair of river otters frolicking along the shore. They dove into the water as we approached and ducked into a den inside an embankment. We could hear them inside, communicating in a language only known to otters, their voices echoing in what was likely a small cave.

As much as the Santa Fe is a wildlife haven, it does have its share of problematic issues and threats. Over the past few years, the river has had chronically low water levels, a result of below average rainfall combined with increased aquifer withdrawals. And still, water bottlers seek to withdraw more water from the river's springs. One company was approved for tapping a side spring in 2000, but in recent years, five more proposals have surfaced for a three mile stretch of river. Opposition has been growing and some proposals have been defeated or delayed, especially in light of historic low water levels. The low water was evident at one rocky stretch where we had to step out of our watercraft and push them along the shallow stretch for thirty feet. And only a quarter mile above the Highway 27 Bridge, a rocky span fifty feet wide completely blocked the river.

The Santa Fe's water quality has become degraded over the past few years, too. Massive algae blooms were apparent, especially near the blockages where there is inadequate flushing. Litter is another issue, mostly during the warm months below the launch for tubers at the privately-owned Ginnie Springs. Despite frequent clean-ups, the amount of bottles and cans (mostly beer) below the tube launch can be overwhelming. Appeals to Ginnie Springs to prohibit disposable containers on the river, especially for tubers, has been unsuccessful, mainly because beer sales are a big part of their business.

One river resident, a famous one who even has a pale ale named after him in High Springs, keeps litter to a minimum in his immediate vicinity. Since 1986, Ed Watts, alias Naked Ed, has taken care of Lily Spring and greeted paddlers in the buff or wearing a loin-cloth. We paddled up the short spring-run, feeling hopeful.

Naked Ed, fully clothed.

We found the bearded naturist fully clothed and sitting beside a fire in front of his palm frond covered hut. The only thing naked was his prominent bald head. Temperatures in the fifties evidently deterred the famous hermit, but he did say he stripped down on a recent cold day at the request of visitors from Michigan who knew of his fame. "I hate to disappoint people," he said. "I've posed for pictures with all kinds of people, even church groups. And a few will actually take their clothes off, too, for a dip in the springs. But if they're uncomfortable with me being naked, I'll slip on a loin cloth, especially if kids are around." I had heard that Ed had a collection of different loin cloths, but he didn't volunteer to show them to us.

 Ed was surprised to see anyone paddling the river given the earlier rain and cool weather and he regaled us with stories of how he prevented people from trashing the springs and turning it into a party spot, and how he was interviewed every semester by University of Florida journalism students—usually pretty young women, he said. But what was really on his mind was the potential sale of the ten-acre Lily Spring property. It has been up for sale for two years for more than $700,000, according to Ed. Ed said he was helping the owners screen would-be buyers. "You can tell if they're serious or not," he said. Of course, Ed would love to continue being the caretaker of Lily Spring if it is sold. He paused, and added slowly, "I'd hate to leave this place."

 Numerous hand-lettered signs posted on trees remind guests of Ed's philosophy of non-judgment regarding nudity—"I'm not qualified to cast the first stone. Are you?" Other signs advocate a respect for nature, and one asserts that "man is the most dangerous animal in the jungle."

 Ed said he loves having respectful and sober visitors, especially "girls in their twenties," although he assures them he is harmless. Still, what would a Santa Fe River Adam fantasize about other than an Eve? Is Ed simply a lecherous old man or some kind of folk hero? Perhaps he is an amalgamation of both.

Ed's public nudity emerged from a childhood disease. He was born with brittle-bone disease and he spent a lot of time in hospitals, becoming accustomed to being naked in front of nurses and doctors. Once he was an adult, after working various jobs, it became dangerous for him to work since he could so easily break bones. He once broke a rib while coughing. He began to receive government disability and wanted to move to a place where he would be comfortable in his birthday suit, and people would be comfortable—or tolerate—him. A 1985 canoe trip down the Santa Fe River turned him on to Lily Spring, and a dire need to clean it up, and so a rent-free arrangement was made with the owners. Ed became the unofficial caretaker. And so a legend—"the wild man of Lily Spring"—was born.

St. Petersburg Times reporter Jeff Klinkenberg penned an article about Naked Ed in 2000. "Ed is a throwback to an era mostly gone," Klinkenberg concluded. "Once every corner of our state boasted a genuine eccentric living in the woods or on the water. But like panthers and crocodiles, few were able to survive civilized Florida. Yet Real Florida hangs on. There are woods and swamps just big enough to harbor endangered wildlife, and a few hidey holes that can shelter an endangered hermit or two."

Several famous hermits and characters in remote places color the pages of Florida's history. On Panther Key in the Ten Thousand Islands, for example, one of the area's most colorful characters once lived—Old John Gomez. Born in 1778, Gomez claimed to have been patted on the back by Napoleon, served as a cabin boy with the pirate Jose Gaspar (Gasparilla), fought in the Second Seminole War with General Zachary Taylor at the Battle of Okeechobee, and operated as a blockade-runner during the Civil War. He named his home Panther Key because panthers would swim to the island and eat his goats. Old John Gomez attracted many visitors and writers to Panther Key until his death in 1900 at age 122.

Another famous Ten Thousand Islands resident of the nineteenth century was simply known as the Hermit of the Ten Thousand Islands. Fiction may have been inserted into legend because the hermit supposedly had a hideaway with slaves and a harem of beautiful women. Can a man be called a hermit if he has a harem? He allegedly captured an occasional white man for prolonged conversation. That part I believe.

The 1850 census revealed that only male hermits resided on Sugarloaf Key in the Lower Keys. One was known as "Happy Jack." Believed to have a fondness for whiskey, he survived by trapping deer and raising fruit. Other colorful Keys hermits of the time included Paddy Whack, Jolly Whack, Red Jim and Lame Bill.

Sir Lancelot Jones was born in a boat in Biscayne Bay in 1898 to a Bahamian mother and former slave father. His father gave his two sons great names so they "would become great men." His brother's name was King Arthur Jones. Lancelot eventually inherited tiny Porgy Key in southern Biscayne Bay and was its only resident for several years. Millionaires, presidents, and celebrities all used him as a fishing guide, but Sir Lancelot reached out to all kinds of people and was considered an expert in marine life. "We would visit him by boat and bring him a key lime pie or ice cream on occasion and he was always happy to visit a bit," my friend Monica Woll of Tavernier told me. "He also came over to Adams Key where I did overnight kids' camps and talked to the students and sold sponges for a quarter! Definitely a highlight of their trip."

In the 1960s, developers wanted to transform Porgy Key into a resort and offered Jones a good deal of money, but he refused. He did eventually sell his 277 acres to the National Park Service to be included as part of Biscayne Bay National Park with the stipulation that he remain as long as he wished. With Hurricane Andrew bearing down on the key in 1992, park personnel forced the elderly Jones to leave and he never returned. Monica Woll recalled visiting him in Miami the day he received Richard Nixon's memoir, personally inscribed to him. Jones passed away in 1997 at the age of 99.

The "wild man of the Loxahatchee"—Trapper Nelson—was a Tarzan-like figure in southeast Florida from the 1930s until the mid-1960s. Often going shirtless (not naked) to reveal his muscular physique and barrel chest, Nelson would entertain visitors with a huge indigo snake draped over his shoulders. He trapped animals for fur and operated a small zoo along the river. His homestead is now part of Jonathan Dickinson State Park.

In North Florida, near Panama City, the first known full-time resident of St. Andrews Peninsula in the twentieth century was a Norwegian-born sailor by the name of Theodore Tollofsen who wrecked his boat on the south bank of Grand Lagoon during a 1929 hurricane. "Teddy the Hermit" decided to homestead and remained until his death in 1954 at age 74. His makeshift shack, mostly erected from driftwood, once stood between campsites 101 and 102 of the current St. Andrews State Park campground.

Along the remote Florida Big Bend Coast, near a tiny outpost known as Spring Warrior, lives a colorful figure named Billy Sullivan, aka "Shitty Bill." In a home-built cabin surrounded by salt marsh just above the high tide mark, Billy built a crow's nest overlooking the prairie-like expanse of cordgrass and needlerush. I once asked the fifth generation coastal resident how he came to be known by his nickname: "When I bought this place, I just was enjoying myself so much down here that my wife come down from Perry and said, 'Billy, when you coming home?' I said, 'Hell, I am home.' So, we worked out a deal. If she wants good cooking, she come see me. If I want good loving, I'd go see her. You know what, I got shit on again. I got too old for the good loving, and she eats every day! And I had to cook for her, you hear? I got the wrong end of the stick. That's why they call me Shitty Bill."

So, given Florida's history of colorful characters, how will Naked Ed stack up? Rather well, I would venture, given his current following. And I wonder, who would follow Naked Ed, if anyone? Could I be the next Naked Ed? I liked the outdoors, I liked company, I liked to gaze upon beautiful women, but going naked was generally reserved for the shower and an occasional private skinny dip. Plus, my wife would divorce me, or worse. After a brief consultation with myself, I realized that a pale ale will never be named after me for my naturist fame.

We bid farewell to this unique river resident and finished our perfect paddle at Rum Island Park. After loading our vehicles, it began to rain again. Perhaps it was the beginning of a Noah-like soaking—the region could sure use it—so we weren't complaining. And if you have an opportunity to paddle the Santa Fe River, regardless of rain, don't pass it up.

Postscript: Tropical Storm Debby bore down on North Florida in June of 2012. Naked Ed's shack was swept away in floodwaters, but the hermit of Lily Spring returned as soon as the waters receded.

If You Go

North-central Florida's Santa Fe River is usually navigable from the U.S. 41/441 Bridge near High Springs to the Suwannee River. The last take-out before the Suwannee is the U.S. 129 Bridge southeast of Branford for a total of 26 river miles. To ensure adequate water levels in the upper river, however, check the Suwannee River Water Management District online gauge at the U.S. 441 Bridge and make sure levels are above 32 feet: http://www.srwmd.state.fl.us/realtimeriverlevels/realtimeriverlevels.aspx. More than three dozen springs flow into the river, some privately owned.

If water levels are adequate, some paddlers enjoy going upriver from the U.S. 441 Bridge to River Rise, about 2.5 miles one way. This is where the river reemerges after flowing underground about three miles in O'Leno State Park.

For more information about the Santa Fe River Paddling Trail, log onto http://www.dep.state.fl.us/gwt/guide/designated_paddle_santafe_guide.pdf.

Suwannee Spring was barely trickling out of its opening during the drought of 2011.

10
Paddling the Low and Slow River of Song

"Having supplied ourselves with ammunition and provision, we set off in the cool of the morning, and descended pleasantly, riding on the crystal flood, which flows down with an easy, gentle, yet active current, rolling over its silvery bed. The stream almost as transparent as the air we breathe; there is nothing done in secret except on its green flowery verges."
>William Bartram, 1773, commenting on a clear Suwannee River

The first thing I noticed about the Suwannee River was that it was low, low and slow, and sporting a clear golden hue when flowing over a sandy bottom. The current at the Spirit of the Suwannee Music Park (River Mile 148.5) was almost imperceptible. Thirty-foot limestone walls—white and pock-marked—bore silent witness to the drought conditions of mid-October, 2011. This promised to be the slowest Paddle Florida trip in its four-year existence. With the west wind blowing fallen leaves on the water, it looked as though the river was flowing backwards! Still, any trip on the famous Suwannee River is special, even one with almost slack water.

  Paddle Florida offers large group trips for paddlers in which food, entertainment, educational programs and transportation are provided. For this initial gathering at the music park, we heard from Charlie Houder, Assistant Executive Director with the Suwannee River Water Management District. "Right now, at this water level, you are essentially paddling through the Floridan Aquifer," he said. "Only groundwater is feeding the river right now. It is essentially a giant springrun."

  Charlie gave us an overview of the Suwannee's water characteristics and current challenges. "We were shocked to learn only a couple of years ago that we're having a water shortage in this area. Everyone once thought the Floridan Aquifer was endless." From various speakers over the course of the seven-day Paddle Florida event to Manatee Springs, the 35 participants learned about springs that had dried up along the upper Suwannee, low water flow and nitrate pollution in other springs, and ways to develop a water ethic to reverse the trend. We would see the problems first hand one paddle stroke at a time, while still enjoying the refreshing springs, viewing wildlife and leaping sturgeon, and trying out the occasional rope swing. At times, silver-haired adults were giggling like children. It was fun to see.

The initial challenge of the trip was the first full paddling day. I was the sweep boat, meaning that I stayed in the rear to help slow and struggling paddlers. We had several beginner paddlers, mostly women who had finished raising families and were now exploring outdoor pursuits. Most had never paddled more than a couple of miles at a time, and now they were faced with a 21 mile day! I employed my best coaching skills and utilized lots of patience as we negotiated several shallow sandbars. I had brought a headlamp and tow belt just in case, but we made it to our spacious camp at Suwannee River State Park before the dinner bell without me having to use either item. We were treated that evening to a special concert by the Big Cypress Bluegrass Band. Besides educational talks, entertainment is a Paddle Florida specialty.

The next day was 25 miles, with some swift shoals just below Ellaville, but paddlers had an optional shuttle at the lunch break. A couple of beginners actually turned down the shuttle. "My husband said I would never make it," said one paddler. "That just makes me more determined to paddle every mile."

Another woman, a more experienced kayaker, added, "My husband supports me coming on these trips because I come home happy. Happy wife, happy life!"

I'm happy to say that all of my "charges" at the rear of the pack made it through the trip with only minimal whining, and they pitched in to pick up trash along the river as part of the Great Suwannee River Cleanup. By the last day, they felt they could climb Mt.

Everest! It was empowering for them and rewarding for me. I received lots of hugs at the end and all of the former beginner paddlers vowed to return for more adventures.

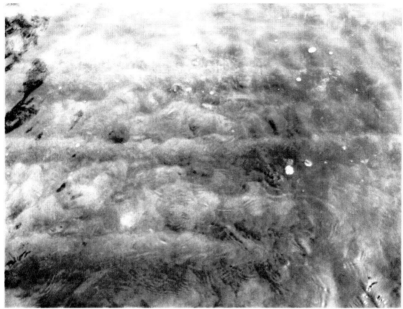

The ribs of a sunken Confederate ship just below the surface of spring run at Troy Spring.

If You Go

Any time of year is good for paddling the 265-mile Suwannee River, even in the heat of summer. And it's not just because of the clear springs that make ideal cooling off spots. Some state parks along the way offer camping and cabin rentals, and several river camps have been set up at ten-mile intervals that include screened pavilions with ceiling fans. The river camps are currently free-of-charge and can be reserved by calling 1-800-868-9914. They even feature hot showers and flush toilets! Paddlers can also primitive camp on sandbars and other public land along the river, but they should first notify the Suwannee River Water Management District for a free special use permit: 800-226-1066 or 386-362-1001.

To learn more about the Suwannee Wilderness Trail, along with local outfitters, log onto http://www.floridastateparks.org/wilderness/. Paddle Florida information can be obtained at http://www.paddleflorida.org/.

For adequate water levels in the upper river between White Springs and Suwannee Springs, the online gauge at White Springs should be above 52 feet, but not near the 77-foot flood stage, either: http://www.srwmd.state.fl.us/realtimeriverlevels/realtimeriverlevels.aspx.

Suwannee Water
Touching the Suwannee
I feel her many springs
Her cypress and limestone
Shoals and high banks.
Touching the Suwannee
I sense her rich history
Dugouts and river boats
Mineral spas and bluegrass.
Touching the Suwannee
I know her troubles
And wonder what people will feel
When they touch the Suwannee
A century from now.

11
Revisiting Rock Island

An island juts from the sea along our Big Bend Coast that is like no other in Florida—Rock Island. This 20-acre chunk of land left over from when sea level rose during the past ten thousand years is solid limestone along most of its edges, and to walk its shores is to visit a moonscape of pocked holes and tidal pools. Live oaks and sable palms dominate the interior and swarms of noisy grackles and wading birds fill their branches. Anyone can visit the island by boat or kayak—it is three miles southeast of the Hickory Mound Impoundment—but camping is limited to sea kayakers doing all or part of the 105-mile Big Bend Saltwater Paddling Trail, managed by the Florida Fish and Wildlife Conservation Commission (FWC).

In the spring of 2012, I joined then FWC trail manager Liz Sparks and a team from Canoe and Kayak Magazine on a Rock Island campout. We had blustery weather on the way, with three to four foot waves lapping over our kayak bows and spray skirts, reinforcing the fact that this trail is primarily for experienced open water paddlers. But once on the island, the wind was welcome since it kept the sometimes notorious bugs at bay. On a 2003 trip to the island in early September, when I was helping Liz finish the trail guide, we called it Biting Fly Island due to the voracious flies, mosquitoes and no-see-ums. And a smaller island nearby was labeled Little Biting Fly Island. Our suffering was chronicled in my first book, *Waters Less Traveled*. But that was early September, hot with no wind. This was April and quite different.

We walked the shores and marveled at designs carved in the rock by ocean waters along with two perfectly round craters about ten feet in diameter. When wet, the pocked limestone has a volcanic appearance, and it is easy to imagine a distant atoll, or maybe one of the Hawaiian Islands. Liz and I had walked these shores nearly a decade ago and they haven't changed much, but we knew sea level would continue to rise and slowly inundate Rock Island, pushing back the greenery until there was nothing but rock and marsh, and eventually a reef. For a few more decades, however—our lifetimes—Rock Island will likely retain a semblance of its current appearance. I'm glad to know it's there for those infrequent stays—for a taste of the wild Big Bend Coast.

Soon after the Big Bend trail guide was finished, I moved on to map the 1,515-mile Florida Circumnavigational Saltwater Paddling Trail for the Florida Office of Greenways and Trails while Liz remained with the FWC to manage the Big Bend Trail and others. Paddlers apply for free permits online to paddle all or part of the trail and utilize some or all of the trail's seven primitive campsites. Since the trail's inception, paddlers have applied for several hundred trail permits. Four overnight trip options are available, or paddlers can choose to tackle the entire trail in one shot.

"The trail remains a niche trail for experienced paddlers," Liz said, "but there are lots of great day trip opportunities for less experienced people. Slowly but surely, more people are discovering this coast. We're trying to help the local communities benefit from sustainable tourism so they can offer better services for paddlers, and we encourage paddlers to support local businesses. For people looking for a real wilderness experience, it's a great trail—rewarding and enjoyable."

In 2013, in a twist of fate, Liz left the FWC and took over my job as paddling trails coordinator for the Florida Office of Greenways and Trails when I took a promotion in the same office. "This is my dream job," she said, perhaps regretting an earlier decision to pass up the job. I was glad life had given her a second chance.

If You Go

Paddling the open waters of the Gulf can be challenging, even for experienced paddlers. And given the remoteness of the Big Bend Coast, it is important that paddlers properly prepare and keep track of weather forecasts. For more information about the Big Bend Saltwater Paddling Trail, log onto https://myfwc.com/viewing/recreation/wmas/lead/big-bend-paddling-trail . The 40-page semi-waterproof trail guide can be ordered for $15 through the website or by calling (850) 488-5520. Reservations are required for the campsites. You can also learn about the Big Bend by viewing the online Florida Circumnavigational Saltwater Paddling Trail Guide. Segment six covers the Big Bend region: http://www.dep.state.fl.us/gwt/paddling/Segments/Segment%20Segment6.htm.

12
The Wacissa's Last Limpkin

"The Wacissa is now, and always has been, a beautiful, clear, spring fed river. In my eyes there is no river any prettier anywhere that I have ever seen."
    Richard Aron Williams, *Wacissa River Man*

At least I found one. One limpkin probing for apple snails along the upper Wacissa River near the headsprings. It was shy, moving deeper into the interior floodplain forest as I approached in my kayak. It was the first and last one I would see on this summer evening of 2012. Was it the last of its kind?

    Four years before, on a warm evening like this one, I found about a dozen along this same stretch. Some were solitary while others were in pairs. A limpkin along nearly every bend. Most didn't seem shy. They probed for snails or perched on logs out in the open. Occasionally, they would call to each other—*krow, krow, krow*. The river echoed limpkin as it had for thousands of years. What happened? What changed in four years time?

Limpkins are intriguing brown and white speckled wading birds that emit eerie calls and clucking sounds. They have specially curved beaks that enable them to probe golf ball-sized apple snail shells, and since apple snails—or *escargot*—are their primary food source, that specialization may have spelled its demise in some areas. If apple snails decline or disappear, so do limpkins, similar to the plight of the endangered Everglades snail kite in South Florida.

Apple snails—and limpkins—may not have disappeared completely from the nearby Wacissa River east of Tallahassee, but kayakers started noticing the decline in limpkin sightings for a couple of years. And soon, biologists with the Florida Fish and Wildlife Conservation Commission (FWC) started noticing, too. What was baffling them was why? Could it be the recent drought? Or vast mats of smothering non-native hydrilla? Water quality? Human disturbance? Predation? The timing of herbicide releases to knock back aquatic plant control?

Limpkins disappeared from Wakulla Springs State Park nearly 15 years ago after occupying the river for thousands of years. They started declining soon after a 1994 flood during the apple snail breeding season. The arrival of invasive hydrilla in 1997 that coincided with a drop in water quality may have provided a final shove. Occasionally, a lone limpkin returns to Wakulla for a rare but brief visit. To lure limpkins back, biologist Jesse Van

Dyke spearheaded efforts to restore the park's apple snail population, and early results were promising. Clusters of the light pink apple snail eggs, often seen on tree trunks and cypress knees, are on the rise. The limpkin remains as a type of mascot for Wakulla Springs, like Henry the pole-vaulting fish, and one of the park's jungle boats is still named after the bird.

The Wacissa's last limpkin in 2012.

Because limpkins are also found in Central and South America and the Caribbean where their numbers are much greater, they are not considered endangered as a species. In Florida—the only state where limpkins breed in the continental United States—limpkins are protected and have been designated a species of special concern. One can occasionally spot them foraging along ponds and lakes around Tallahassee and along the St. Marks River just below Natural Bridge.

Is there hope for limpkins on the Wacissa River?

"The limpkins have come back because we stopped eating them," one lifelong Wacissa resident said with a chuckle last year at a public rally of river lovers opposed to Nestle's plans to tap the river's springs for bottled water. Limpkins and other wild birds were once heavily harvested throughout Florida during lean times before conservation laws were enacted and enforced. Limpkins were nearly eradicated as a result. Today, the causes of decline are not so easy to pinpoint.

But limpkins aren't the only reason I venture to the Wacissa River. I return to the Wacissa River time and gain for inspiration and spiritual sustenance, especially on a weekday or early Sunday morning when few others are on the water. The Wacissa is like an old friend, one I've grown up with since moving to Tallahassee at age eleven. When I launch my kayak in the clear water of the headsprings and begin paddling into that wide panorama of beauty, I am at peace. I feel alive. It's that simple.

While on the river, I acknowledge the many wading birds and other creatures. I feel privileged to share the stream with them, if only for a short while. Great blue herons stand sentinel-like. An eagle peeps from a tall cypress while a trilling kingfisher zooms past. Otters and turtles poke their heads up while an occasional alligator or water snake slides off the shore. In the evenings, owl calls echo across the marshy vista and wading birds begin to roost. As the sun dips low, I know it is time to leave, but I vow to return again and again.

Do the Wacissa animals know me? I fantasize that they do, but it is unlikely. If I lived along the river and ventured to the shore or paddled the river daily, they would know me, and hopefully not feel fear. But as an occasional visitor in a kayak, they simply know my kind—people in those funny boats. I hope that we, paddlers, have a good reputation with the river's critters.

I feel for a place like the Wacissa. I fret over changes or proposed changes that threaten the equilibrium. I want the mullet to keep leaping and limpkins to continue probing for apple snails and otters to play unmolested. I am aware that centuries-old cypresses along the shore have watched humans come and go for generations, and so I will one day leave this place, never to return. I hope that day is in the distant future for the Wacissa pulses through me. I have been baptized by its waters and I hope nothing can drain its lifeblood from my veins.

I pray that whatever caused the limpkins' decline will reverse itself—with our help, if necessary—and scores of the brown and white birds will again find the Wacissa a suitable home as they have for millennia.

River otter along the upper Wacissa River.

If You Go

The upper Wacissa River can easily be accessed from Highway 27 between Tallahassee and Perry. At the Highway 59 junction, head south four miles to the four-way stop in the town of Wacissa. Keep driving south about a mile. When Highway 59 forks to the right, keep going straight until the road dead-ends at one of the Wacissa River headsprings.

The upper Wacissa is an easy river to paddle upstream or downstream. Weekends can be busy and an occasional airboat can shatter the quietness. Three businesses near the headsprings rent kayaks and canoes.

**13
Paddling among Giants**

"I have stood beneath the great redwoods of the California coast and felt the awesome majesty of their age and size. One walks quietly and with proper reverence through these groves, as in a cathedral. Their cypress cousins here in Apalach are neither so big nor so old as the virgin redwoods, but quite as fascinating. They seem less aloof and demanding, more a part of the daily life of the rivers and ponds on which they flourish. Canoeists reach out to stroke the sculptured knees. White herons and egrets arrange themselves artistically in the crowns. Kingfishers plunge from lookout branches. Owls sit motionless, staring down the passerby. Even the dead cypress are impressive. Great hollow trunks, riddled with woodpecker holes and draped with Spanish moss, stand miraculously upright when only a few slim segments of the decaying wood will reach to the ground."
> Betty M. Watts, *The Watery Wilderness of Apalach, Florida,* 1975

I was in a wild mood. Not for rambunctious partying, but for wild Florida, where a leafy canopy over a winding waterway wraps you in a tight cocoon, allowing your spirit to expand.

And so I slapped a kayak on my car and headed southeast. I passed any number of choices closer to my home—the Gulf near the town of St. Marks, the middle section of the St. Marks River above Newport, the coastal bays and inlets around the St. Marks Lighthouse, and the lower Aucilla River to the Gulf. Instead, I turned north off Highway 98 onto Powell Hammock Road and headed into one of the most uninhabited regions of Florida. I wanted to paddle among giants, the ancient cypress near the Slave Canal entrance along the lower Wacissa River. The loggers of a century ago somehow missed a side stream where a half dozen massive trees still tower over a wild swamp. They didn't have satellite imagery then, and this place was hard to reach.

Georgia Ackerman paddling the Avenue of the Giants.

Most of the trees are not hollow or twisted, like so many remnant old-growth cypress seen along our rivers. These are hardy specimens worthy of a saw mill, only I'm glad they were spared when nearly everything else in the area was girdled and cut. Perhaps the loggers were wrapping up their work when they glimpsed the big trees through the foliage—"Damn, we've been in this swamp long enough. Let's get the hell out of here!"

A friend calls it the Avenue of the Giants, named after the famous 31-mile portion of old Highway 101 through the northern California redwoods, featuring the famous drive-through tree. The Florida version stretches only a quarter mile or so, but it is worthy of almost two miles of one way paddling to get there.

After miles of driving on jarring limerock roads, a white cloud billowing out from my car like a fast-moving dust devil, I reached Goose Pasture at a wide spot on the lower Wacissa River. Apalachee Indians, and those before them, used this spot for millennia, and now it is a public campground. A couple of friendly families hung out at the landing, radio blasting. Toddlers in sagging diapers splashed in the water while older children dipped minnows with tiny nets. I extended my greeting as I unloaded, knowing I would not linger long because the wild was calling. I was soon floating atop swirling eelgrass, surrounded by singing birds. Schools of gar and mullet swam past. Turtles plopped off logs as I entered the first of many canopied braids. Ahh, the wild.

I like to come alone when I am in a wild mood, when I want to paddle among giants. When I am with others, it is usually just a cursory look at the trees as we are on the way to the Slave Canal or to Half Mile Rise—the largest of the lower Aucilla's sinks. But the trees themselves are a worthy destination. Who glances at a giant sequoia on the way to someplace else?

 Small alligators, half the size of my kayak, slid in quietly. I passed a statue-like yellow-crowned night heron. There were more Suwannee cooters on logs than I could count, but no people. None. Motorized craft are rare in these shallow side channels where navigation can be confusing and snags are just below the surface. And most paddlers do this section on weekend mornings as part of longer trips. So, late afternoon—weekend or not—is perfect.

 After one wrong turn and a correction, I reached the trees. I slowed my paddling, savoring. Vines of fox grape, poison ivy and Virginia creeper wrapped around gray trunks and branches. Buttresses and roots were like massive knuckles gripping the shoreline, holding on through hurricane and flood. Protruding cypress knees resembled weathered Tyrannosaurus teeth. Being alone, it felt like a hallowed place. Mute elders of another species emanating power and silence.

 I lingered, glancing at the dipping sun over the horizon, gauging my time. On my return trip, I startled a couple of alligators. During warm weather, they become more active late in the day—dinner time—only I knew I wasn't on the menu even after a five-footer suddenly popped up just inches from my paddle before splashing away. Still, I was glad when the river opened up and I spotted Goose Pasture, the shoreline bathed in yellow light. The wild had filled me, but it was not a permanent home. I would need to work and play and socialize and do all those things humans do for a well-rounded life. Still, that occasional pull is hard to resist. Maybe one reason the giants still stand.

Large cypress along the Avenue of the Giants.

If You Go

The easiest way to reach the lower Wacissa River and Goose Pasture is to drive on Highway 98 and turn north on Powell Hammock Road. If traveling east on 98, this is the third road on the left past the Aucilla River bridge (about two miles). Signs point to Goose Pasture. Travel north on Powell Hammock Road about four miles and turn left on a graded limerock road and follow signs to Goose Pasture.

Once exploring the many side streams just south of Goose Pasture, take along a compass and GPS unit to help you find your way back. Be sure to take a GPS reading of Goose Pasture before you embark. Once the river widens about a half mile before the Slave Canal entrance, the Avenue of the Giants is a side stream on the left, marked by an old growth cypress. GPS coordinates for the entrance in decimal-degrees are N30.1860, W-83.9707. Aerial photos can aid in navigation.

For more about the Wacissa River Paddling Trail and the Wacissa River Slave Canal, log onto http://www.dep.state.fl.us/gwt/guide/designated_paddle Wacissa_guide.pdf. My book, *Wild Florida Waters*, features a chapter about the Slave Canal. The nearest outfitter is The Wilderness Way, located 30 miles west of Goose Pasture at Wakulla Station, 850-877-7200. Take along a guide or a knowledgeable friend for the first time or two you explore the area. The current below Goose Pasture can be swift in places, so you need to be a strong paddler if you plan on returning to Goose Pasture by paddling upstream.

14
Florida's Remotest Spot

"...the mosquitoes here are the worse than I imagined such pests could get and give us no peace day or night. Some of my men who have worked along the East Coast say that if all the mosquitoes at Jenius, Ft. Pierce, New Smyma and Jupiter were collected in one locality they would feel ashamed in comparison with this Cape Sable multitude. If there was any way of escape I don't believe I would have more than three men left by tomorrow night."
William J. Krome, 1903, surveying a potential route for the Keys Railroad

Ryan and Rebecca Means of Tallahassee enjoy exploring wild places. But the adventuresome couple took their passion a step further by beginning Project Remote, an effort to identify and document the remotest locations in all 50 states. They have already traveled to and documented most of the eastern states, and their progress can be tracked on their website, http://remotefootprints.org/.

The Means' work with a scientific team that includes Ryan's father, renowned wildlife biologist Bruce Means, at the Coastal Plains Institute based out of

Tallahassee. The non-profit organization, begun in 1984, has primarily focused on wildlife research and education, but Remote Footprints has expanded their scope to include the exploration and documentation of remote areas and to facilitate relations between people and wild places. "We took a look within ourselves and realized that the conservation of remote and roadless areas is paramount to the conservation of biodiversity," Ryan Means explained. "We also believe there are thousands, if not millions of Americans who hunger to have true wilderness experiences in their lives, and hearing, seeing and smelling the roar of nearby fossil-fueled civilization detracts greatly from our ability to do so."

Rebecca, Skyla and Ryan Means in North Carolina, photo by Mary Buckner.

Means recently guided a small group of us by kayak and canoe down the lower Wacissa River to the

Aucilla River at Half Mile Rise, about thirty miles southeast of Tallahassee. One of Florida's wildest river systems, this lower section branches out into a confusing network of braids that includes some pullovers of snags and even a small set of rapids.

Roads, or the lack of, are the determining factor in gauging the remoteness of an area. Even a tortuous, unpaved road, such as the one leading to Half Mile Rise—our take out—counts as a passable road, which leads to the question, how remote is the lower Wacissa River? We didn't see any roads or other humans once we left Goose Pasture, so it seemed wild and unmarred—and it is certainly scenic with clear, spring-fed water and large trees—but as we approached Half Mile Rise, we could hear a distant limerock mining operation. To our surprise, despite the fact that most of the area is in public ownership, it turns out that the lower Wacissa doesn't rank that high. In any given spot, a road is less than a mile-and-a-half away. "Almost nobody understands just how many roads there actually are," Means says.

With their expertise in both biology and GIS mapping, Ryan and Rebecca are doing something unique in calculating the remotest (i.e. the most roadless) single point in each state, and mounting expeditions into each for its proper documentation. The initial calculation is a long process greatly aided by GIS computer software. The Kentucky Remote Spot calculation, for example, took weeks to determine. Both a scientific journal article and popular book about Project Remote will result from their efforts, along with an awareness of the damage that roads can cause, especially in conservation areas. Appropriately, the exact coordinates for each spot won't be given out to the general public. Having people tromping through the wilderness to the remotest locations could cause an undue impact.

The Means' expeditions, usually by backpack but sometimes in combination with watercraft, include their pre-school age daughter, Skyla. "She [Skyla] has taught us that we as a family are limited only by our imagination—she is game to do just about anything!" Means says. "As an added bonus, we hope our work will inspire families like us to get outdoors and Go Remote themselves."

So, what is the remotest spot in Florida? It is the Marquesas Keys west of Key West. The islands are 25 miles from the nearest road and, preliminarily, this appears to be the remotest location in the lower 48. The remotest spot on the Florida mainland turns out to be just north of Cape Sable in Everglades National Park, what appeared on Google Maps as "a conspicuous white strip running roughly north to south sandwiched by blue ocean to the west and green mangrove to the east." In other words, a secluded beach.

That spot is seventeen miles from the nearest road, although motorized watercraft are currently allowed in the federal wilderness area. This situation regarding motorboats prompted a discussion between Ryan and Rebecca regarding the best way to document the spot.

"We had a decision to make," Ryan wrote in an account of the trip. "Do we take our 18-foot motorized john boat or do we paddle kayaks or a canoe into the spot? After long deliberation, Rebecca and I decided that it would be acceptable to use any of the travel methods we would have at our disposal while Remote Spotting as long as it was lawful and part of the local MO for travel. Plus, we imagined the irony and disappointment of doing a 10-day paddle voyage through the Ten Thousand Islands region only to reach the remote spot and find motorboats anchored to shore and people on the beach who spent hours instead of days getting there. Furthermore, we had challenging logistics to contend with of Remote Spotting in all 50 states on limited time and funding. We decided to take the motorized aluminum john boat sitting in our yard that had been collecting acorns and leaves."

They found the remotest spot on the last day of 2009, their first of the 50 states. Mid-winter is usually the best time to enjoy the Everglades as far as insects swarms are concerned, but at sunset, the area lived up to its reputation. "Just as the last of the daylight faded, the notorious Everglades mosquitoes came out in force," Rebecca wrote. "The middle of winter in south Florida means nothing to mosquitoes. Florida is endowed with more mosquito species than any other state in the U.S. The ferocity and density of the mosquito clouds around us rivaled any I have ever felt in Alaska. I think all 80 Florida species converged on us that night."

There is often a price to pay for going remote.

It seems appropriate that the Everglades ranks as the remotest spot in Florida. The region worked for the Seminoles. They survived there—their last stronghold—because of its remoteness and difficulty in navigation. And desperadoes often found refuge there as well and in the adjacent Ten Thousand Islands. No one had GPS or satellite imagery then. Detailed maps of the region were non-existent. You just had to know the place and know where to hide. And, at that time, a dugout canoe was the primary means of transportation.

Besides the vast mangrove maze and sawgrass swamp of the Everglades, I'd be curious as to the remotest spot along a Florida river, a place miles from a road and reachable by kayak or canoe. That would be a fun project to pursue.

15
Onward, to the Pinhook!

Bald eagles were our guides as we made our way down the lower Aucilla River and began skirting through a maze of tidal creeks and coves to the Pinhook River. I was with a loose-knit group of experienced paddlers who, appropriately, call themselves the Loose Cannons. It's not a club; just friends wanting to paddle together. And they gave me a good excuse to paddle to the Pinhook River in the heart of the St. Marks National Wildlife Refuge.

The Pinhook is perhaps the wildest small river we have in our region because the upper reaches are only accessible by kayak or canoe, and then, it is preferable when the tide is up. Limestone covers the shallow river bed and you can smell sulphur, so perhaps its origin is a sulphur spring or two.

In the 1800s, people on the run found the Pinhook to be a suitable place to hide, especially during the Indian removal period of the 1830s when Native Americans were being forcibly sent to Indian Territory, now Oklahoma. "Grandpa Ace Brown, an Indian renegade [Muscogee Creek], along with his wife Margaret and children had lived beside the Pinhook River in thatched houses," said Richard Aron Williams in *Wacissa River Man*. "The Pinhook winds in from the Bay, first through saw grass and then through dark, mysterious water with palm trees and palmettos lining the banks amid other trees and brush. It is beautiful and has an aura of something happening, or that did happen long ago. It would be a beautiful place to live. Mama was living with her parents on the Pinhook River, near the Aucilla River when Daddy met her. I can picture my mama living there on the west side of the river with her brother and sisters. It had to be a peaceful, though hard life, with little outside interference unless a fisherman came by. When you are quietly boating on the Pinhook a calming, almost euphoric feeling comes over you. I can imagine the winds howling off the Bay through the trees and water roaring along the river in bad weather. I think about the hard life of my Mama. About all they had for food was meat they killed, flour, salt and a few things they could grow. In spite of the hardships they did choose a beautiful river on which to make their home."

Since it was my idea to paddle up the Pinhook, I was elected as trip leader, even though I had never attempted the paddle before. So, I downloaded an aerial Google map, logged coordinates into my GPS, checked the tides, and we embarked on a perfect winter morning. A few no-see-ums stirred, but nothing else marred the day, not even the small alligator that jumped off the bank and startled one paddler. That was to be expected. It was one of only two alligators we spotted, and the other one—a fat five-footer—was sunning and refused to budge as we passed.

The most striking part of the journey was when we rounded a bend and saw where the wide, marsh-lined Pinhook suddenly narrowed and was bordered by arching sabal palms and steep limestone banks. Even the Highwaymen artists couldn't have dreamed up a wilder Florida scene.

Alligator along the Pinhook.

We lunched on a refuge-built wooden bridge along a former rail line that is now a premier hiking and bike path. We shared brownies, hot tea and other goodies until, almost begrudgingly, we embarked on our return trip. The tide was starting to ebb, that being our main time clock.

So, if you want to dream up a perfect Florida outing, factor in 70-degree temperatures, a light breeze, a wild place, and—most importantly—good friends.

If You Go

To find maps for paddling the Pinhook River, check out segment five of the Florida Circumnavigational Saltwater Paddling Trail: http://www.dep.state.fl.us/gwt/paddling/Segments/Segment5/Segment5.htm. Map 4 provides entrance gps coordinates for the Pinhook River, N30.0996 W-84.0157 in decimal-degrees, as well as information about the lower Aucilla River. Coordinates for the wooden bridge over the Pinhook about two miles upstream are N30.0996 W-84.0157. Aerial photos are also helpful in navigating the many tidal creeks in the area. Some open water paddling experience is recommended. Long-distance paddlers can utilize a primitive campsite near the Pinhook bridge after obtaining a permit from the St. Marks National Wildlife Refuge, (850) 925-6121.

16
Night of the Attacking Mullet

"Of all the fascinating things about Wakulla Springs and the fenced-in sanctuary that enclosed it, two dominated: a sense of the uncaged wild immediately at hand plus the faint, pleasure-accenting uneasiness that it brought; and the contrasting sense of ease and elegance delivered by the lovely old white lodge with the red-tiled roof."

    Al Burt, *Al Burt's Florida*

Unfortunately, I wasn't present for the night of the attacking mullet. The event, now part of Wakulla Springs lore, ranks up there with Tarzan, the Creature of the Black Lagoon, and the Wakulla Lodge fire of 1943. It happened in 2011 during the after-dark jungle boat ride as part of the annual Wakulla Springs Wildlife Festival. Biologist Dana Bryan was leading the tour.

    "We were nearing the end of the tour in the back jungle when we came upon maybe two hundred mullet in a tight area," Bryan recalled. "The water was churning with jumping mullet. Well, they must have panicked because they started leaping and hitting the boat and then jumping into the boat. Everyone was screaming. Even people at the lodge heard the screams and wondered what was going on. Mullet were flopping everywhere, people were trying to throw them back in, and at the end of the tour, fish scales and mullet blood were all over the floor."

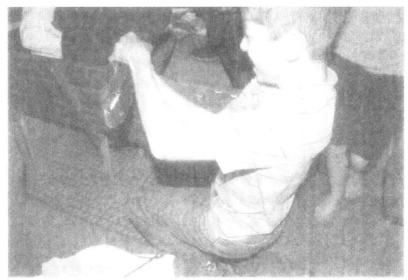

Boy rescues a mullet from the boat bottom during the "attack". Photo by Meghan Mesler.

I joined Bryan on the 2013 tour on April 20th, hoping for a repeat performance. One elderly couple sitting in a front row seat recalled the attack. "I had three mullet jump into my lap!" the woman said. "I was one of the ones screaming." Since no one was hurt during the mullet attack, even though one woman was hit in the head, I guess the couple came back for another adrenalin rush.

Once on the tour, as stars and planets emerged and cypress trees transformed into dark silhouettes, we spotted a barred owl, a manatee, numerous bats, yellow-crowned night herons, and alligator eyes that glowed red when hit with a flashlight beam. Bullfrogs croaked from within bulrush and katydids sang from treetops. When we reached the back jungle, I volunteered to shine a flashlight from the boat's bow to serve as a type of headlight for boat driver Jake Hines. I soon spotted a few dozen mullet moving at a rapid pace. "Mullet!" I cried. "Lots of them. They're luring us in for the kill."

People chuckled nervously and swung flashlight beams to the water. A few silvery mullet leaped, but to my disappointment, their numbers weren't great enough to launch themselves wildly at the boat and passengers. No kamikaze attack on this night. But the night tour was still memorable and I vowed to make it an annual tradition. And maybe I'll get lucky one year and have a mullet or three jump into my lap!

If You Go

If you want to attend an evening boat tour on the Wakulla River and take your chances with flying mullet, check out the annual Wakulla Springs Wildlife Festival every April, http://www.wakullawildlifefestival.com/. The tour is from 8:00 pm to 9:30 pm and is labeled the "Sounds of the Night" tour. There is a small fee. Numerous other tours and events are offered.

17
Bringing Back the Holy Grail of Springs?

"The future of our springs depends on public advocacy. We can no longer afford to buy the false dichotomy that would have us choose between a healthy economy and a healthy environment, for the former will surely wither and die without the latter. Nothing less than the soul of Florida hangs in the balance."

      John Moran, nature and springs photographer

The fish in the Wakulla Springs "fish bowl" were legendary. For decades, African-American boat drivers would glide over the gin-clear water of the spring bowl and call up the bullhead catfish in a sing-song, gospel-like voice. Hundreds would begin following the boat as if marching to orders. An old post card called it "the fish parade." Of course, food the drivers dropped into the water was the main incentive for the fish, but it was easy to gaze down as a child and imagine that the guide had magical powers over the finned creatures, especially when he glided above an exposed log and began to call to a small bass named Henry. "Come on Henry, come to the pole! You can do it, Henry. You don't want to disappoint these good folks. Come on, Henry, jump the pole!" And Henry, or Henrietta, would indeed brush against the pole in a flipping motion, most likely to dislodge parasites. "Hey ya'all!" the driver would call out excitedly. "Come on, do it again, Henry! Hey ya'll!"

Henry, "the pole-vaulting fish," and the fish bowl were mainstays of the Wakulla Springs glass-bottom boat tours. But when nitrogen levels began skyrocketing in the mid-1990s and the spring became increasingly murky and algae-covered, the fish largely disappeared. And the glass bottom boat tours became rare occurrences due to dark water. That's why I jumped at the chance in June of 2013 when the spring suddenly cleared enough for the glass bottom boats to run again. Water clarity was at about 80 feet, not exactly gin-clear, but we were still able to gaze in awe into the 120-foot abyss like in days of yore. Mastodon bones, though algae-covered, still lay across the bottom in one spot, along with the hollow "Tarzan's log" that Johnny Weismuller used to swim through during the filming of two Tarzan flicks in the 1930s. After the movies, hundreds of teenagers, including myself, used to swim through the log when it was closer to the swimming area, a rite-of-passage for generations of local boys.

The missing attraction on the contemporary glass-bottom boat tour was fish. No catfish. Not one. Only a few mullet and panfish. And neither was there "Henry the pole-vaulting fish." Most of the eelgrass around the headsprings was missing, too, smothered by invasive hydrilla that first showed up in the late 1990s.

What happened to the fish? No one can say for sure. Scientists do know that certain forms of algae can be toxic to fish. Also, algae robs water of oxygen, and fish need oxygen to survive.

With the decline of fish and the Wakulla ecosystem in general, monthly—and more recently, weekly—wildlife surveys over a twenty year span revealed a disturbing trend. Alligators and nine birds species, including moorhen, anghinga, snowy egret and wood duck, have been dropping in number. As far as birds go, only the pied-billed grebe numbers are on the rise.

But the news at Wakulla Springs isn't all doom and gloom. Manatees have arrived in increasing numbers as if answering a silent distress call. They numbered around 60 in the winter of 2012/2013, putting such a dent in invasive hydrilla populations that herbicide spraying was skipped for the first time in years. And even though an estimated 460 tons of nitrates annually flowed through Wakulla Springs for the past few years, nitrogen levels are slowly dropping as Tallahassee implements a $227 million renovation of their sewage treatment plant. Effluent from the plan is discharged at a massive sprayfield, and dye studies proved a direct underground connection to Wakulla Springs.

I learned more about the nitrate reductions on a four-hour overland tour led by springs expert Jim Stevenson. Tallahassee's sewage plant was one of several stops on a tour that included several area lakes, sinkholes, springs and swallets (sinks that swallow streams)—

following the path of surface and groundwater to Wakulla Springs.

"It took some public pressure, but we're very proud of the city for stepping up," said Stevenson of the sewage plant improvements. "We're seeing the nitrates drop at Wakulla Springs and we attribute that to what they've done."

Jim Stevenson at Ames Sink on the Wakulla Springs Overland Tour.

Stevenson also credits the city and county for efforts in reducing pollution from stormwater runoff, but more steps are necessary. He urges homeowners to pump out septic tanks every five years, reduce water waste, and curtail lawn fertilization. Stevenson was successful in convincing Tallahassee Community College to stop fertilizing their grassy expanses except for ball fields, and the Florida Department of Transportation also stopped fertilizing 218 miles of roadsides in the Wakulla Springs basin. "Sometimes you just have to ask," he said. "A little education can go a long ways."

Stevenson and other members of the Wakulla Springs Alliance are also urging county and state officials to address the estimated 9,000 septic tanks in the Wakulla Springs "Primary Springs Protection Zone" south of Tallahassee. While most septic tanks in the region do a good job of reducing health risks associated with human waste, much of the nitrogen seeps directly into the aquifer and eventually discharges at Wakulla Springs. "We have always thought about springs as the beginning," Stevenson said. "But we've learned the spring is the end of the pipe."

To help remedy the situation, activists propose that neighborhoods close to Tallahassee be hooked up to the improved city sewage plant while more distant neighborhoods be connected to small-cluster low-nitrogen wastewater systems using proven technology. Obviously, some subsidization would need to occur for low income residents since all of the options bear a cost of several thousand dollars per household, and many families in the region are barely scraping by, living in decrepit mobile homes and small houses along wallowed out unpaved roads. I know this for a fact because I live only six miles north of Wakulla Springs on an unpaved road, and as testament to the karst nature of our surroundings, we have sinkholes on three sides that are directly linked to the springs. I used to think that as long as my septic tank didn't back up or gurgle out foul liquid in my drain field or produce a nasty smell, it was rendering waste harmless, but now I know different. My septic tank is polluting the refuge of my youth, the landmark water feature of our region, the Holy Grail of springs. And I need help fixing it.

No one knows the exact point where nitrate levels drop enough in Wakulla Springs so that algae dies off, native eelgrass begins to out-compete invasive hydrilla, and fish and wildlife rebound. "That's because we've never brought back a spring," Stevenson said. "But we need to keep trying. Wakulla Springs is worth the effort."

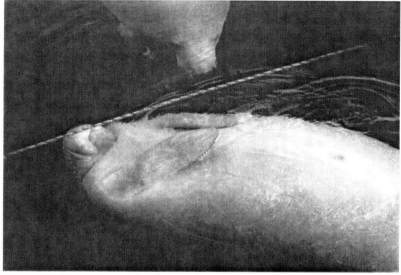

A manatee ducks under the swimming area rope at Wakulla Springs State Park.

If You Go

Educating the public is what the overland tours are about. They usually occur on the third Saturday of the month fall through spring. To sign up, call 926-3376 or log onto www.palmettoexpeditions.com. Most of the registration fee is donated to the Wakulla Springs Alliance and Friends of Wakulla Springs.

18
Paddling the Swift Ochlockonee from Dam to the Bay

Tornado warnings, fierce winds and sheets of rain greeted more than thirty kayakers and canoeists at Ed and Bernice's Fish Camp along Highway 20 twenty miles west of Tallahassee. The camp was the gathering point for Paddle Florida's second annual Dam to the Bay Paddle on the Ochlockonee River in early March—six days, 76 miles—and by first impressions, it would be a trip of the damned. But we knew favorable weather was in the forecast. So, we squeezed tents under pavilions and stayed dry the best we could. We even started a fire along the edge of one pavilion. Sleep was difficult that night as rain battered the tin-roofed shelters.

The next morning was blustery, but skies were a deep blue. Bald eagles, ospreys and vultures soared while long garfish near the water's surface seemed especially frisky. Was this gar mating season?

In the afternoon, a few of us stopped at the historic Langston Ferry site. The ferry ran from 1876 to 1929 in the days before the Highway 20 Bridge. People who approached from the west side of the river often blew a conch shell to alert the Langston family on the other side to bring the ferry boat. Charges ranged from a nickel to twenty cents, depending on the load size. The Stoutamire family manages the site and they have erected a covered bridge Methodist chapel across a side stream with memorial benches honoring family members who have passed. Appropriately, they have included a conch shell on a chain so guests can give the traditional horn blow for the ferry. A year later, some of us stopped at the site, but posted signs kept us in our kayaks. After all, it is private property.

In 2010, Reddick Langston wrote this about the ferry, operated by his grandfather of the same name: "In order to ferry the barge across the river against a swift current, a 5/8 inch steel cable was stretched across the river and secured on each side of the river bank. Next, two chains were attached to the barge, one toward the front and the other toward the rear. The chains were attached to steel rings which encircled the cable, allowing the barge to be secure against the current of the river and at the same time to slide along the cable at the barge was moved back and forth across the river.

"Power to push the barge forward was achieved by a long pole placed against the river bed. As the operator applied pressure to the pole, he would move the length of the barge, repeating this procedure until reaching the river bank, at which time 'gang planks' were placed from the barge to the river bank, allowing vehicles to move on or off the barge."

Nearing our campsite at the Huey P. Arnold Park after 16 swift miles, two boat anglers told me they had rescued a man in a yellow kayak who had tipped over after hitting a snag. He made a total of three people who took unscheduled swims on this first day due to snags, swift current, and the narrow and twisting nature of the river in sections. The river often moved us along at five miles per hour with only light paddling.

That night, I dreamed of torches floating down the waterway, and these flickering lights soon turned into paddlers. My thoughts focused on how rivers were much more than paths that nature made for water to flow downhill. So many species have evolved in and along these waterways that they are corridors of life and therefore, fascinating places to paddle. The Ochlockonee is especially attractive, flowing through lands now protected by various local, state and federal agencies and sensitive private landowners, keeping the river's natural systems largely intact. And it is almost completely overlooked by most people in Tallahassee. This reverie was interrupted by shivering as night temperatures dipped into the thirties. Why hadn't I brought my long johns or fleece sweat pants!?

Monday, our second day, warmed to short-sleeve shirt weather in the 70s. The swing in temperatures was astounding. Ronny Traylor, our trip leader, showed us a small riverside cabin since he knew the owners.

Humorous and philosophical signs covered the aged siding. How many backwoods cabin owners post quotes of Albert Einstein?

A side slough filled with gnarled old-growth cypress added to our day's explorations. These trees were spared the logging boom of the 1920s due to their twisted nature and low wood value. They seemed to emanate age, respect and quiet. Unlike most of the river trees, the green cypress needles weren't popping out yet.

Owl cries echoed across our camp at the remote Whitehead Lake Campground. The river hadn't crested from the heavy rains and there were worries that our boats near the landing would be washed downriver, so we tied them to trees. We also heard that flooding was possible at Ed and Bernice's Fish Camp and our parked vehicles could be threatened. Paddle Florida coordinator Bill Richards vowed to keep abreast of the danger and rush to the camp to move our vehicles if necessary. We tried to push the threats out of our mind around the fire as we told stories and jokes and sang a round of "Grandma's Feather Bed" by John Denver. We also humorously observed the various ways people roasted marshmallows. In summary, we easily entertained ourselves.

The landing at Whitehead Lake is separated from the campground by a side stream that must be waded. Overnight, the stream rose from being ankle deep to past our knees, and the water was cold!

Ben Oneal and Jimmy Sanders of Eastpoint, deadhead loggers, were launching their boat at the landing. The duo pulls out submerged cypress and longleaf pine logs in the river after receiving expensive permits from the state. While the practice often disrupts fish habitat, Ben maintained they are "cleaning up what our ancestors left". About ten percent of log rafts from the logging boom days sank in the river and sloughs and every flood uncovers more logs. Wood from these old-growth trees can be highly valuable once sawed into boards for siding and mantles.

As the day warmed, we zoomed down the swift-flowing river, witnessing the ever emerging colors of spring. Besides popping leaves, blooming wild azalea and titi drew our attention. Hawks cried, eagles soared—another perfect day.

Exploring Mack Slough along the Ochlockonee.

Arriving at the Mack Landing Campground just after one o-clock, many of us had time to explore the tortuous and swift-flowing Mack Slough, another wonderland of cypress and tupelo trees. After dark, Mack Slough was the backdrop for the entertaining and edgy tunes of local musician Grant Peeples. Paddle Florida is known for providing educational lectures and musical entertainment at their evening camps. On this trip, we also learned about water management, wetlands mitigation, bee keeping and other area paddling trails. Sopchoppy musician Frank Lindamood provided entertainment at another campground.

Wednesday morning began smoothly as the fast current carried us to our lunch stop at Pine Log Campsite in Tate's Hell State Forest, and some people explored the old-growth cypress along Hitchcock Lake (another side slough). After lunch things went topsy-turvy. Several people were confident they could find the Womack Creek Campground, our destination, so they left before our trip leader on the ever widening river. Perhaps in the spirit of Cebe Tate, for whom Tate's Hell is named, they became lost.

High water had opened several side sloughs that resembled the main channel. Plus, a southerly wind and an incoming tide slowed the current to a near standstill. This resulted in several confusing channel choices and some people chose poorly. Ronny Traylor and I chased down one party, but two others didn't find their way to camp until later in the afternoon. In the future, we vowed to be more careful in this section.

After a short day's paddle to Ochlockonee River State Park on Thursday, we had an oyster feast. There's nothing better than a fresh bushel of oysters steamed over a fire. Some paddlers showed off their oyster shucking expertise, to the delight of many waiting with crackers and hot sauce. A perfect setting for a perfect party. In the afternoon, time was spent either snoozing or walking along high river banks beneath arching live oaks or through some of the best maintained longleaf pine flatwoods in the state. Red cockaded woodpeckers, an endangered species, are in relative abundance along with an array of songbirds, deer and white squirrels.

Approaching the white sand beaches of Bald Point State Park along the Gulf of Mexico the next morning, we navigated a maze of oyster bars with their associated crying gulls and terns. Ospreys soared and fish popped. Salt air filled the southern breeze—an ideal place to end a six-day paddling journey from the dam to the bay.

If You Go

For more information about the Lower Ochlockonee River Paddling Trail, log onto: http://www.dep.state.fl.us/gwt/guide/designated_paddle/Ochlock_guide.pdf. Ed and Bernice's Fish Camp can be accessed by driving about twenty miles west of Tallahassee on Highway 20. The camp is along a paved road a quarter mile southwest of the bridge. Signs clearly mark the way. There are no outfitters along the river, but canoes and kayaks can be rented at The Wilderness Way ten miles south of Tallahassee (850-877-7200).

To learn more about Paddle Florida, log onto www.paddleflorida.org. For more information about Ochlockonee River State Park, easily reached by vehicle along Highway 319 just south of Sopchoppy, log onto http://www.floridastateparks.org/ochlockoneeriver/default.cfm.

19
100,000 Paddle Strokes on the Thirsty Apalachicola

"When he was growing up, the Apalachicola river and bay were a certainty in his life. The river was sweet and clean. The bay was full of oysters. They would always be that way. They were bountiful and eternal. A Panhandle boy could romp and fish and do as he pleased, and nobody would suffer and nothing would become scarce. Ecology had not been discovered, or invented. As far as the environment was concerned, life was a fairy tale without a big bad wolf."

    Al Burt, *Al Burt's Florida,* speaking of long-time
    Apalachicola resident Bobby Howell

Thick fog. Whiteness. A blank slate. I paddled this same Apalachicola River two years before, 106 miles from Jim Woodruff Dam to Apalachicola in five days as part of the annual Apalachicola RiverTrek. And like the previous trip, I had joined a group raising money for the Apalachicola Riverkeeper, and raising awareness about the river's plight. But the thick fog at the launch had already made it different.

Maybe fog is the ideal symbol for adventure. You can't see far ahead. Obstacles come into view quickly—shoals, islands, rocks, bridges, rusted heaps of steam ships along the opposite shore. Stop for a moment and your companions are lost in the mist. Only their excited voices carry. Swallowing fog. Engulfing.

That's how the 2012 Apalachicola RiverTrek started—in thick fog. Eleven participants embarked from Chattahoochee for a five-day kayaking trip to Apalachicola and they were soon lost in the mist. Wondering what lay ahead.

Included in our group was a *Tallahassee Democrat* reporter, Jennifer Portman. Her front-page article about the trip had already helped to raise its visibility. Donations poured in to the tune of almost $18,000. In addition, Rob Diaz de Villegas with WFSU television was documenting the entire trip and a WFSU camera man was aboard a boat with Riverkeeper Dan Tonsmeire. Another paddler, Leon County Commissioner and Florida Association of Counties president Bryan Desloge, also helped to raise the trip's profile.

As fog began to clear, turtles slid quietly off logs. Great blue herons lumbered away. Gar and other fish kissed the moving plane of water. Crows—a murder of them—called raucously.

As anyone knows who has been following the Apalachicola saga, the river has been starved of freshwater by Alabama and Georgia, causing fish populations and other organisms to decline and bringing about the near collapse of Apalachicola Bay's oyster fishery. Yet, the river is still beautiful and dynamic, and it has the strongest flow of any Florida waterway. And part of the Apalachicola's wonder lies beyond its immediate shores.

For a late morning break, state park biologist Mark Ludloe toured us through a remote section of Torreya State Park along a narrow creek that had carved a deep path through limestone bedrock. "It's a Grand Canyon in miniature," he said. A highlight was a small cave that we could stoop down and walk through, thus the reason we were asked to bring flashlights.

Mark showed us a torreya tree, the region being the only place in the world where the conifer grows in the wild. A fence of chicken wire surrounded it to keep out deer, but it couldn't keep out the fungal blight that strikes down each tree before they reach maturity. First documented in the 1930s, there is no known cure for the blight, although torreya trees planted outside of the region are currently blight-free. Scientists consider the torreya the rarest and most endangered conifer in the world. "It's the California condor of trees," Ludlow concluded.

Once a hiking trail is put in place, this remote and unique area of the park will be open to the public.

We spent the afternoon cruising along the Apalachicola's high bluffs. The bluffs have served as a fitting backdrop for a colorful cavalcade of history—Native American canoeists, Spanish explorers, English traders, escaped slaves, American gunboats, paddle wheelers, steamships, barges, and now—again—paddlers.

The river has been a silent witness, always flowing, carrying travelers and trade goods, feeding villages, nourishing souls.

As evening hues shone on the massive Alum Bluff across from our sandbar campsite, biologist Helen Light lectured about the importance of the river floodplain and normal freshwater flows. According to Light's decades-long field research, it is not just Apalachicola Bay that the river feeds. During high flows, the river sends water through the many sloughs which, in turn, spreads water into the wide floodplain, nourishing a myriad of fish, invertebrates and other life forms. The river's floodplain, the largest in Florida, is what feeds vital nutrients to Apalachicola Bay. Stop or diminish this cycle and the bay and the system's incredible biodiversity suffers. Already, the spawning area of the endangered Gulf sturgeon was above water for the first time in known history.

Plants and trees suffer, too. Light's research indicates that the chronic low water levels have resulted in the loss of four million floodplain trees, primarily Ogeechee tupelo that require wet conditions. According to Light, erosion of the river channel due to the lack of sediment laden water released from the dam, among other reasons, has also contributed to the cutting off of river sloughs.

Just after sunrise, we climbed the steep Alum Bluff to meet a highly enthusiastic field biologist with the Nature Conservancy named Annie Schmidt. The Conservancy is doing an impressive job of restoring upland areas to the native longleaf pine/wiregrass ecosystem and their results should give hope to other restoration efforts throughout the South. "I love my job!"

she said as she bent low to examine an expanse of bright yellow flowers known as coastal-plain honeycomb heads. Lower to the ground were blue curls, a blue/purple flower, and there were the tall purple spires of blazing star. Clumps of tall wiregrass, a natural bunchgrass, was spread out in an impressive array.

Speaking of biodiversity, Bryan Desloge found an impressive venomous snake by almost stepping on it—a brightly colored copperhead across from Alum Bluff. The Apalachicola is one of the few places in Florida where copperheads can be found and Bryan discovered it while changing clothes near our campsite. "My political career is over," he joked after being interviewed on camera by Rob. "I described how I pulled down my pants and jumped back from a snake!" Copperheads, especially, are known for striking out immediately when threatened, although they often inject little venom for these warning bites. Fortunately, this snake was non-aggressive.

Southern copperhead along the Apalachicola River.

Later in the trip, Bryan would scare up a large cottonmouth by sitting on a rotten log during a lunch break. It was an unusual tan/orange color and I pondered whether we had found a new subspecies. But, alas, after checking with renowned herpetologist Bruce Means, I learned that the snake was merely stained with river mud. "When I catch one and wet it, the natural colors come out," he said.

We cruised toward Bristol that morning along more high bluffs. Small streams gurgled as they cascaded through carved notches in the rock and clay.

During the long days of paddling, we watched numerous bald eagles, including two adults with a juvenile eagle. I assumed fishing lessons were occurring. I also paddled into a headwind alongside a migrating monarch butterfly. Once the wind died, the monarch flew faster than I could paddle.

Floating, paddling, floating, paddling, it takes hours to make a twenty-plus mile day, and so the river was the moving canvas of expression and life. Even with a group of eleven paddlers, you can find yourself alone on a long day. You may have paused to observe a bird or to take a pit stop, and the others have suddenly become distant specks. Thoughts, songs, and memories come more readily. Soaring bald eagles seem to have added relevance. Did the eagle circle overhead just to check me out, sun glistening on white head and tail, or was it simply a random passing? Other questions come to mind: does the Apalachicola River have a soul or spirit as some native people believe? Or, does the river somehow synergize a collective type of energy from the many life forms that depend upon it?

Besides the risk of becoming a backwoods philosopher, there are other inherent risks in paddling the Apalachicola River for five days. Simply, you begin to care. Deeply. And a certain level of frustration emerges. It's like falling in love with a person who has a life-threatening illness, a disease that is curable but with remedies that seem just out of reach. For solutions to become accessible, it means moving a collective mountain of attitudes that border on ignorance and uncaring.

The upriver masses of people may have heard something about oysters dying, but what does that have to do with lush green lawns in Atlanta? Or golf courses, water parks, swimming pools, fountains, and artificial waterfalls? And what about South Georgia and North Florida farmers who water and water and water without employing readily available techniques that use precious water in the most efficient manner? To save the Apalachicola River and Bay, it will take education, political will, and more people who care, no matter where they live.

Cynthia Barnett said it best in her soon to be classic book about the vital necessity for wise use of water resources, *Blue Revolution: Unmaking America's Water Crisis:* "Water is much more important to our future than oil. That's because there are no alternatives to it, no new substitute for life's essential ingredient being cooked from corn, French fry grease, or algae. …

"Using water ethically isn't difficult. It's revolutionary only because it's so different from the way modern America relates to water. But this revolution isn't big, costly, or bloody. It's a revolution of small technologies over mega-waterworks. It's a savings of billions of dollars in infrastructure and energy costs. It's as painless as floating on your back in an azure spring. Call it a blue revolution."

Barnett described how some of the world's cities have cut their water use by half. We can do the same. Upriver homeowners collecting rainwater and landscaping with drought-resistant plants, farmers employing drip irrigation practices and utilizing computerized soil sensors to know when to water, and common sense conservation practices by all parties, including Floridians, can help save the Apalachicola River and Bay. Not to mention more water releases by the Army Corps of Engineers.

We took frequent swims on sandbars during hot afternoons and we climbed the four-story Sand Mountain, created by the Army Corps of Engineers during their multi-year dredging operations. The practice ceased in 2002 because it wasn't cost-effective, especially in light of the environmental harm it was causing.

On the way home, my body felt like it had been through a washing machine and spit out. Participant Rick Zelznak, spouse of trip co-organizer Georgia Ackerman, estimated that we had done 100,000 paddle strokes. I wondered how much longer I could do these marathon type trips, where every day is twenty-plus miles, and paddling into a headwind against the tide on the last day made it seem like forty. I turned to participant Alex Reed, who was preparing for an Iron Man competition where she will run a 26-mile marathon, bike more than a hundred miles, and swim two-and-a-half miles—all within 17 hours! "How do you feel?" I asked.

She shook her head. "I'm whooped." Then, she added, "But it's a good type of tired."

That made me feel better. I knew the soreness and stiffness would soon be replaced by memories of glinting kayaks, soaring eagles, and warm camaraderie. A moment in time that can never be re-created again, not exactly, for every trip has elements and conditions that make it unique.

By publicizing our trip, we were including people in on a little secret—this is a dynamic place to boat, paddle, fish and explore. The mountain of resistance will only move if people go beyond just enjoying oysters on a plate. By watching sunsets and moonrises, spotting otters, bald eagles and jumping sturgeon, the Apalachicola becomes more than a name. It becomes a series of images that has sounds, smells, feelings… Simply, it becomes alive. And it is pleading for our help.

Here's what some of my paddling companions had to say about their experience:

"It took us five days to paddle the river, but it would take weeks, maybe months to explore every creek, swamp, or slough that connects with it, or every forest or bluff alongside it. Natural treasures are scattered about its basin like pennies in the crevices of a couch. I've paddled the whole river, and I feel like I've only just gotten started to get to know the Apalachicola. And I want more people to get to know it, too, to recognize it as a destination and recognize its importance to the people of our area."

Rob Diaz de Villegas

"RiverTrek 2012 was an accidental cause for me. I thought I was just joining old friends and meeting a few new ones to paddle for a few days. What I didn't expect was to fall in love with the Apalachicola River. Through educational seminars given by experts and thoughtful conversation among fellow paddlers, my care and concern for the river basin—its history, its wildness, its majesty—grew and grew over the five days we floated along. Like many, I was aware of the 'water wars' between Florida and Georgia and I had some idea of the plight of the oystermen in Apalachicola. But what I didn't understand is that it is not just a political battle, but an ecological one. When you actually get to see the disconnected sloughs and swamps, the old high-water marks, and the overgrown sandbars, you understand this is a slow-motion train wreck; all the more sad and tragic because we can watch it happen and because we can do something to stop it. This is the mission of the Apalachicola Riverkeeper."
    Micheal Taber

"RiverTrek was a break from the everyday world where you learned to appreciate the creature comforts of home but yet yielded to the whims of the outdoors. The cooler nights and mornings required communal fires and coffee where stories were told. Dedicated scientists took time to educate us on the river, its flood plain and the habitat that depended on its flow. So many interconnected parts to this Apalachicola River it makes your head spin. The politics of state, Federal and local interests colliding to squabble over this precious river, yet it seems so simple to solve when you watch a few eagles soar or gaze at the ancient cypress. I hope and will work for our children being able

to enjoy this treasure from the tupelo honey, abundant wildlife and the oysters."
    Mike Mendez

"It is difficult to wrap my head around the complexity of the situation sometimes. We spent five days enjoying the majesty of this river—her power, her ecology, her inhabitants—and yet, from the river's edge, it is difficult to see the demands placed on this amazing natural resource. The river is facing challenges from unfettered growth and development to antiquated irrigation practices to interstate commercial demands to recreational interests to ecological needs. It seems that this river has been stretch beyond her capacity for quite some time. How long do we have to ignore the need for conscientious management of this river? Please join the fight to conserve this American Treasure."
    Alex Reed

"After my first through paddling trip on the Apalachicola in 2011, I discovered this quote by Stephen Jay Gould: 'We cannot win this battle to save species and environments without forging an emotional bond between ourselves and nature as well - for we will not fight to save what we do not love.' During RiverTrek 2012, my emotional bond with this wilderness place, the mighty river, and my fellow paddlers grew deeper. We must fight to save Florida's Apalachicola River."
    Georgia Ackerman

"From the seat of a kayak, the Apalachicola seems more remote than it appears on maps that show scant cell phone coverage amid a wide swath of green. Paddling its entire length brings into close focus the uncertain future of a fragile environment and a way of life as endangered as the rare species found only here."

  Jennifer Portman, *Tallahassee Democrat*, 11/4/12

If You Go
  The Apalachicola River is usually best paddled in the fall and early winter when water levels are at seasonal lows. Numerous sandbars are exposed for rest stops and camping and the current, though always fast moving, is easier to negotiate. For best paddling and camping conditions, the USGS river gauge at Chattahoochee should be below 44 feet: http://waterdata.usgs.gov/fl/nwis/uv/?site_no=02358001&PARAmeter_cd=00065,00060.

  Drinking water can be obtained at several parks along the route, although grocery stores would require walking a couple of miles or more, so it is wise to bring enough food for the entire trip. The Apalachicola Blueway guide includes a data book of rest stops, parks, campsites and points of interest, along with seven detailed maps. To access the guide, log onto http://www.dep.state.fl.us/gwt/guide/Apalachicola_River_Blueway_complete.pdf.

20
Devon Creek Magic

Perhaps the most breathtaking of the Apalachicola River tributaries is Devon Creek when the water is high enough to venture in with a kayak or canoe. Just off Owl Creek—the entrance nearly obscured by branches—the waterway is completely canopied by cypress and tupelo gum branches. In spring, a season when water levels are usually high enough, the bright green sprouting leaves make for a spectacular contrast to the grays and browns of the curving tree trunks.

I first found Devon Creek by accident more than thirty years ago on a canoe trip down Owl Creek with my mother and a friend. Once we entered the leafy corridor, we were entranced. We spoke in hushed tones as if loud voices would break the magical spell. Occasionally, we pointed out cypress knees and roots that had artistic shapes. Finally, as light faded and the creek narrowed, we reluctantly turned around, vowing to return one day.

A couple of years ago, I revisited the creek and found the "cypress angel" about a half mile in. Her upper trunk had been shorn away and then twisted in a large halo-like curve over what appeared to be a head, with perfectly spaced "eyes" pecked by woodpeckers. Branches protruding from the middle of the trunk resembled arms. She stood silent, resolute, a living statue.

And I wondered, was it one storm or several that created her, or was it lightning, shooting through the trunk in a ragged bolt, a searing sculptor's knife? Whatever natural forces were at work, the resulting "angel" was now a thing of beauty and mystery to behold, perhaps standing only until the next hurricane or lightning bolt struck. I like to imagine her as watching over this special place deep in the Apalachicola floodplain, greeting the rare human visitor with an air of quiet intrigue.

If You Go

The easiest way to reach Devon Creek is to launch at the Hickory Landing Campground (part of the Apalachicola National Forest) on Owl Creek. Paddle downstream towards the Apalachicola River about a half mile and look for the Devon Creek opening on the left. GPS coordinates for the opening in decimal-degrees is N29.9799 W-85.0186.

If you want to explore the Apalachicola River and its tributaries, check out the paddling trips offered by the Apalachicola Riverkeeper: http://apalachicolariverkeeper.org/4th-saturday-paddle/.

21
Dry Creek Sunday

Our caravan of vehicles, topped with festive-colored canoes and kayaks, drove past several busy country churches on an October Sunday morning. Cool temperatures and clear skies made it a near perfect day for an outing, and southern Jackson County near Marianna was a much anticipated destination.

We turned down unpaved Mystery Springs Road, a name that conjured up all kinds of pleasant images, and soon launched on Dry Creek. The privately-owned access remains open as long as users are respectful. Kudos to the landowner. A warning sign at the put-in read, "Keep Area Clean Or It Will Be Closed."

Dry Creek is a misnomer. It is spring-fed and rarely, if ever, dry. The water is clear, cool, and sacred feeling.

After passing a large spring known as Black Hole, one fed by other nearby springs, we soon pushed through a thick stand of bulrushes, led by a knowledgeable guide, fortunately. Various branches of the creek then merged together to form a watery tunnel beneath arching cypress, gum, maple and other trees. A living cathedral! Excited voices quieted. Sunlight flashed silver through the leafy dome above.

The winged angels of birds sang as we floated for miles on a ribbon of liquid glass over a pure sand bottom. The sermon on this day was in the symbolism, the beauty and purity, the silence. Move through life with little worry. Live simply. Appreciate beauty and companionship. Commune with Creator. Lilies of the field had been transformed into brilliant red cardinal flowers blooming along moving water. A parable for the ages.

By early afternoon, we came to the State Road 73 Bridge, our destination. I felt refreshed, innocent and child-like. Eternal.

Sunday revival on Dry Creek.

If You Go

The best way to explore upper Dry Creek is to hook onto a scheduled trip with the Apalachee Canoe and Kayak Club. Membership is a whopping $5 per year. Here's their website link:http://www.clubkayak.com/acke/. Since the upper launch is sketchy and on private property, one can more safely paddle upstream from the Highway 73 Bridge. The section of Dry Creek below Highway 73 to the Highway 280A Bridge is occasionally blocked by snags, depending on water levels and the efforts of local volunteers to keep the waterway open. The section from Highway 280A to the Chipola River is generally open. Of course, the 51-mile Chipola River Paddling Trail is well mapped and is a state paddling trail, featuring 63 identified springs and some small caves. It even features a small shoal known as "Look and Tremble Falls." To learn more, log onto http://www.dep.state.fl.us/gwt/guide/designated_paddle/Chipola_guide.pdf.

22
Panhandle Perfection

Sometimes I like mellow streams where you can float and paddle and even close your eyes to swirl in the current with no worries, listening to birds and the river's song. The Florida Panhandle's lower Blackwater River is one such waterway. A highly popular river in summer and on warm weekends, I chose a Monday afternoon in April. Perfect.

The folks at the Blackwater Canoe Rental were accommodating, and they loaned me a serviceable sit-on-top kayak—perfect for floating and jumping out on the numerous brilliant white sandbars for which the river is known. Despite its name—Blackwater, or the original *Oka-lusa* (water black) in the Muscogee language—the water was a transparent golden-brown. Most the stream flows through undeveloped lands of the Blackwater State Forest and Blackwater River State Park, core areas of the largest contiguous longleaf pine/wiregrass ecosystem left in the world. "A forest like this is rarer than a tropical rainforest," says Callie DeHaven of the Nature Conservancy. The water seeping from this forest is as pure as they come, merely tinted with tannins from leaves and roots of shoreline vegetation. No wonder the Blackwater River is so popular.

"I've been on all the rivers around here and this is still my favorite," said Paul Harville, a long-time employee at the outfitter. The business is open year-round, seven days a week in all types of weather. The only time they close is when the river is at flood stage, a rare occasion.

Tampa Bay Times reporter Terry Tomalin paddled the river for three days in single digit, nearly record-breaking winter weather in 2012. Sane people slept in warm beds miles away. "Lying awake, waiting for morning, I wondered if spinal fluid can freeze," Tomalin wrote, "for it felt like every time I moved my backbone was about to snap. After hours of silent suffering, daylight came, but brought no relief. Everything was frozen, including camera and phone batteries, gas canisters and hatches to our kayaks, containing all our food and water, which was now turned to ice."

Those types of trips make for more interesting adventure stories, but what about the perfect days? I don't often write about perfect trips on perfect rivers. …it was sunny, beautiful, and the water was refreshing… Snooze. Surely scary rednecks, snakes, alligators, tipping over, storms, bone-chilling cold and such make for exciting stories. But the Blackwater is worthy of mention because it is one of those rivers where you can have a perfect trip when not too crowded—or too cold. River Zen at its best.

Other exceptional Panhandle rivers—all of which have similar tannin-tinted waters— include the Perdido, Coldwater, Juniper and Shoal. All have inviting sandbars, although the Blackwater has the largest number.

If You Go

The navigable portion of the Blackwater River is 31 miles long. Numerous access points enable one to easily pick and choose desired sections. Not surprisingly, the upper river is narrower with high banks and swift current, requiring more expertise. The lower river is generally suited for beginners. Primitive camping is allowed on sandbars along the river, and Blackwater River State Park has a full-service campground. The nearest towns of any size are Milton, about 15 miles to the west, and Crestview, about the same distance to the east.

To learn more, log onto http://www.dep.state.fl.us/gwt/guide/paddle.htm

23
Bedouin Kayaking

Maybe when I retire, I'll try Bedouin kayaking. That's paddling weeks and months at a time without worry, pushing oneself when the urge strikes, and taking it easy at other times. A wanderer on the water instead of a desert.

I came up with the term when I met up with my friend Tommy Thompson after he roamed the Big Bend Florida Coast by kayak for three weeks one summer. "It was the best vacation I ever had," he said. "At first, I paddled some long days, making miles, but then I started slowing down and feeling like a Bedouin." Bingo. Bedouin kayaking.

Maybe I'll try the Bedouin kayaking lifestyle by paddling the 1,515-mile Florida Circumnavigational Saltwater Paddling Trail from the Alabama border to Key West to the Georgia line. I wrote the guide and mapped the trail for three years for the state, and still help keep the guide up to date, but I have never paddled the nation's longest coastal trail in its entirety. I paddled sections, and ventured out in various types of motorized watercraft with public land managers for other stretches.

The most unusual boat I took was with a ranger from Honeymoon Island State Park. He took me out in a World War II type landing craft that could fit a large pick-up. When we landed on spoil islands that were available for camping, the front of the boat dropped down on shore and we walked on land like General Douglas MacArthur in Pacific island photo ops. In marshy areas, I tried airboats, wearing ear protection, of course. In calm water, airboats can be like magic carpet rides that roar. In choppy conditions, they jar passengers like no other. I lost both arms of my sunglasses on one trip, the tiny screws shaken loose by the bouncing boat.

In the Chassahowitzka National Wildlife Refuge near Homosassa, the manager decided to take his entire staff out in two airboats since "we haven't been out of the office in six months." I silently apologized to the paddlers holding their ears when we passed. "I'm one of you!" I wanted to shout. "I'm just here because it's my job." The trade-off of taking motorized watercraft was worth it. That's how I was able to firm up numerous rest stops and legal campsites with land managers. Some day, I yearn to visit them all by kayak in one shot, but until then, I'll have to satisfy myself with short trips, and by following the progress of Bedouin kayakers on the trail.

Jodi Eller of St. Augustine was the first woman to complete the Circumnavigational Trail and the eleventh paddler overall. She paddled most of the trail in 2008 with husband Matt Keene, the first "thru paddler" of the trail, and she completed the remaining segments in late 2013.

"This trail is amazing," she said. "It goes through so many different ecosystems. How the beaches change along the trail is just incredible. The trail made me a stronger paddler and it also redefined who I am in a way, bringing me back to the essence of being human. It's a powerful experience to go through."

Jodi Eller paddling in the Everglades, photo by Matt Keene.

She experienced "perfect water conditions" during her last segment from Flamingo to Everglades City through Everglades National Park. "This was a day where there was no wind," she said. "Everything was glass. There was nothing on the horizon, so the clouds were mirrored on the water in front of you. So, you would gaze out and everything just looked like sky. Every blade dipping into the water, you were pushed forward towards… almost like an infinity. There was nothing to pinpoint, to focus at. You were just paddling out into the clouds. To me, it was the closest feeling to a heaven. I imagined Morgan Freeman walking across the water in all white."

Paddling into heaven… That's enough to make you want to embark on a paddling journey.

Of course, there was the post-adventure adjustment period that nearly every wanderer must endure. Jodi summed it up best: "I went through this transformation, physically and emotionally, but when you come back to the same house, the same job, the same friends and same family, it almost feels like it never happened. You have these bits and pieces of these memories that could be a dream. I still have the memory and the sadness of not being out on the trail. It's a very humbling and gratifying feeling that I finished it, but it still feels like 'Did that just happen? Did I just do that? Was that really real?'"

One young man I vicariously followed along with was Tallahassee native Daniel Alvarez, whom I've known since he was a boy. Alvarez did more than just paddle the Circumnavigational Trail. In June of 2012, the then 31-year-old "recovering corporate lawyer" embarked on a 4,000-mile solo kayaking journey from the Canadian border at Angle, Minnesota to Key West. He called it "The Heart of America Paddling Journey."

The herculean journey so intrigued outdoor enthusiasts that he was the top vote-getter for a $10,000 adventure grant from *Outside* Magazine. Because the route covered so many areas, Alvarez chose to promote four environmental organizations while he paddled: Friends of the Boundary Waters Wilderness, American Rivers, Gulf Restoration Network, and the Florida Wildlife Federation. He also touted water conservation efforts through his online journal and at press conferences along the route.

"I want this trip to be more than just my fun adventure," he said. "The wilderness has already given me so much. I want to give back." Alvarez has an extensive outdoor resume. He is a "triple crowner," meaning he has completed America's three longest backpacking trails: Pacific Crest, Continental Divide and Appalachian. Throw in the Southwest's Hayduke Trail, and Alvarez's hiking mileage totals 9,000 miles. For the Heart of America journey, he traded his hiking staff for a kayak paddle. "The Appalachian Trail is like a hiking college," he said. "There are two thousand people out there learning how to hike. But few people were out kayaking like I was, so I had to learn while I was doing it. I didn't have much experience with sea kayaking before I started."

Daniel Alvarez taking a break from his journey to give a talk in Tallahassee in 2013.

The muscle strains, sore hands, occasional cuts and, on one occasion, a swelled foot from leeches, was all part of the experience. "You just have to jump in and get a little scarred up," he said. "I don't want to end life with a perfectly good body." And even though kayaking was a different adjustment for his body, Alvarez learned that the endeavor required the same mental fortitude as long-distance hiking. "The biggest challenge is with your mind," he said, "To try to keep positive and focused."

Alvarez found that the main difference between sea kayaking and backpacking is that a sea kayak can hold more gear than a backpack, something he learned to relish. "At first, I brought lightweight backpacking foods," he said, "But I soon learned that extra weight in a kayak wasn't a big deal, especially after the portages."

Alvarez writes a popular blog on his journeys, predictablylost.com, and he honed his writing through long stretches of hardship, adventure, incredible beauty and introspection. Here is part of his journal from June 11th, standing at the northernmost monument in Minnesota:

"I thought about the Boundary Waters and Lake Superior, about the Mississippi and the Gulf, about the Everglades and Florida Keys. I thought about the people I'd meet, the unknown faces turned friends, and the stories I'd hear. I thought about icy water, the sun beating down overhead, and waves rushing over the bow. I thought about it all, standing there captured by my imagination, unable to move until rain began falling around me. It soaked into my shirt and ran down the brim of my hat.

"'Go,' the world said. 'Quit imagining and find out.'"

Alvarez found the Boundary Waters to be challenging. Storms whipped up the huge lakes like oceans. Along the aptly named Massacre Island, wind and waves drove him into rocks. Then, he spilled. "A moment of lost focus," he wrote. "A wave crashing over my deck. The shore leaping closer. The sound of my paddle blade scrapping across a rock. The weightless lift of a second wave. The world spinning sideways. The groan of plastic slamming rock. The desperate need to feel land underneath my feet. The snap of my spray skirt. The rush of water spilling into the cockpit. The weight of the boat as I pulled it on the shore. The sudden calm just two feet away from chaos.

"I stared at the waves from a rocky slice of shore. The forest leaned over me, crowding me, making me feel claustrophobic. I could only hope the wind would change. Until it did, I could not leave."

Some parents would be wracked with worry, but Carlos Alvarez and Anna Lee had a different approach. "I am very proud of Daniel because of this and for who he is, regardless of this journey," Carlos Alvarez said. "I think life is about following your passion and contributing to the well-being of us all. This journey combines all of that. Without a doubt there is a part of me that worries about his journey, but that worried part is dwarfed by the part of me that would worry if he was not following his passion…

"I visited Daniel on the Pacific Crest Trail after he had been out for several months and he wasn't the same person I knew. He could hear things I couldn't hear, and see things I couldn't see. It was amazing to see the transformation."

Anna Lee added, "Life lived in some safe cubby and working to obtain some status quo is not truly lived. When Daniel is challenging himself he is the most happy, so I encourage that. I have every confidence in his abilities. He is an intelligent, thoughtful and strong-bodied young man. Now is the time in his life to pursue such endeavors as this paddling journey. Later, he can laugh and enjoy his memories in a rocking chair somewhere."

Just before the winter solstice, I caught up with Alvarez on his Heart of America journey more than six months after he had embarked. He was paddling out of New Orleans when he answered my battery of questions via e-mail. True to his nature, he took the historic portage between Lake Pontchartrain and the Mississippi River because he "felt like paying homage to the city's founding history."

Alvarez was accustomed to portages. He did several through Minnesota's renowned Boundary Waters Wilderness, the longest being eight-and-a-half miles, but none compared to the infamous Savanna Portage along the East Savannah River, the main impediment between the Mississippi River and Lake Superior. It was several miles long—no one is sure of the exact mileage any more. Once cursed by French canoe traders commonly known as voyageurs, the portage hadn't been attempted for years, possibly even decades. Daniel found it to be "savage"—choked with thick brush, fallen trees, beaver dams and gripping mud, and plagued by mosquitoes and leeches.

"No one goes back there, voyageurs died back there, piles of goods were left in the mud and abandoned back there, so getting the chance to cross it was special," Daniel said. "I felt like I was completely on my own and venturing into a complete unknown. I knew it would take all my will, all the things I had learned along the way, everything I had to make it across a place no one thought was passable."

In the midst of the crossing, Alvarez had another surprise, an incident he wrote about in his blog: "A blur of brown movement slid into the grass and disappeared. I crept closer and a bobcat sprung away in two quick leaps. I'd never seen an animal move that fast. Its muscles exploded with such power and grace that I wondered if it were a ghost. I looked around, suddenly conscious of the wild surrounding me, of how rare man's footsteps were."

After three days in "Hell's playground," his emergence from the portage "felt like bliss." He was soon on the mighty Mississippi River, and he would follow this famous water trail for more than three months. "The Mississippi leg was amazing because I got to experience the commerce running through the middle of the country first hand. The barges grew and grew, from one or two, to fifteen, to 42 barge giants with a bigger mass than a super Walmart. Then came the saltwater freighters near New Orleans that made even the 42-barge tugs look tiny. It is wild to experience that from the seat of a small 17-foot kayak."

And what was the most surprising thing on his kayaking odyssey? "Even as accents changed from Minnesotan to Midwest to Southern and food changed from wild game to BBQ to gumbo, people have remained incredible straight through," he said. "It is refreshing to know how many wonderful people there are out there, especially when you usually only hear about the few bad ones."

He often stayed with people he met on the trail and in trail towns, something that requires trust on both sides. He is comfortable being alone for days on end, but he also relished human company. People rarely stayed strangers for long around Alvarez. And he stayed with new-found friends along the trail for both Thanksgiving (in Memphis) and Christmas. It was all part of the "trail magic" of which long-distance travelers often speak. "Those kind of travel experiences restores our faith that we're all really good people deep down," he concluded. "I don't want to live in a world where you can't trust somebody."

One key to Alvarez's success in long-distance non-motorized travel is that he embodies a "live-in-the-moment" state of mind. That means being open-minded and flexible. He often doesn't plan where he will camp—he just finds a suitable spot, which sometimes means he paddles after dark. "It's a bit like playing musical chairs and finding there are no chairs left," he said. "You just have to keep going until you find a suitable spot, but I enjoyed paddling at night most of the time." That attitude is, perhaps, the essence of Bedouin kayaking.

A scary moment occurred while paddling at night on the Mississippi River. He was crossing the river after determining that the lights of a tugboat and barge were about two miles away when suddenly he was blinded by a spotlight from the tugboat. "I thought, 'this is it. He's closer than I thought, and they can't stop or turn suddenly. I'm dead. This is how it will end.' And I had promised so many people that I would try to be safe." He paddled like crazy, trying to avoid the inevitable, when the beam flicked off. The barge was still about two miles away.

Alvarez consulted with me about the Florida Circumnavigational Trail, but he rarely stayed in the designated campsites. "I usually just find a nice beach after dark," he said a bit sheepishly. "No one has ever bothered me."

And while he doesn't claim to have had a "cosmic" experience on his trips, Alvarez does cite an unaccountable and incredible feeling of bliss and peace at the end of each journey. And on the Heart of America paddling journey, he began to rethink his decision to forego being a lawyer. A friend from law school paddled with him for five days in the Gulf and she had just landed a job with the Natural Resources Defense Council to fight for protection of marine mammals. When they would see leaping dolphins, Alvarez would joke, "Those are some of your clients paying you a visit." More seriously, it caused him to consider pursuing environmental or immigration law, something more closely akin to his passions.

When Alvarez reached the southernmost point in Key West nine months after his start in Angle, he shocked everyone, including his parents, when he decided to keep going! "I realized I wasn't dreaming big enough," he said.

His plan was to finish the Circumnavigational Trail and to keep going up the East Coast to New York, paddle up the Hudson River and connect to the Great Lakes, eventually end up again at Angle, Minnesota, which he did on October 26 as soon as there was a break in the snowy weather. One should never be surprised by the impulsiveness of a Bedouin kayaker.

.

While en-route along the East Coast, Alvarez further explained his decision to make the loop in an article he wrote for Outside Magazine's website: "I had a thousand reasons why it wouldn't work. I wasn't ready to go back. I didn't have another grant to cover my costs, just a thinning bank account and a credit card. My body felt as worn as my equipment looked, full of ripped seams, scratched plastic, and rusted metal. Winter would freeze Minnesota's lakes in seven months and it took me nine to reach Key West. The only research I'd done was chat on docks with power boaters, glance at a map, and figure they get those saltwater freighters into the Great Lakes somehow.

"'I wish I could do it,' I thought to myself. 'But...'

"It's the same thing people say to me when they hear what I'm doing. 'I wish I could do that,' they say again and again. I've heard it on every trip I've ever taken, always followed by a parade of excuses.

"'If I were younger...'

"'If I didn't have my career...'

"'If I only had the money...'

"People always sound like they don't quite believe their words and they're convincing themselves of the truth. I'm never sure what to say back because I think the truth is that it's easier to blame the world than yourself, that there will always be excuses not to go if you want them, that we're trying to rob ourselves of the decision, but that's a hard truth and most people don't like to face it. I know I didn't. I met a one-legged hiker on the Appalachian Trail. I finished the Continental Divide with a 72-year-old. I swapped stories with a one-handed man who celebrated Lewis and Clark's anniversary by trying to paddle up the Missouri River. They had excuses, too."

At talks he gave along the Heart of America journey, Alvarez had this advice for members of the audience: "Take a moment and think of some adventure you've always wanted to do and just go do it. There's never a right moment. There will always be a thousand reasons not to do it, and you'll never have it all figured out. You just have to take the leap!"

It is difficult for me to say, because it's just another excuse, but I may have to wait a few more years to take the leap.

24
North Florida's Botanical Eden

"Torreya State Park runs a gamut. It is full of bewildering variety in its lichens, ferns, mosses and deeply green. If the Great Smoky mountains of Carolina were scooped up and deposited in the tropics they might look this way: tangled, dense, a mixture of plain maples and exotic palms, of pale hepaticas and vivid pink pennyroyal, cloud-brushed treetops and brilliant cardinals streaking from branch to branch."
Gloria Jahoda, *The Other Florida,* 1967

North Florida's remote Apalachicola bluffs and ravines offer more than adventure and wilderness exploration. I usually arrive like a pilgrim drawn to the sacred. The land features and botanical wonders are so unique that some local residents have gone so far as to claim it was the original Garden of Eden, the one where Adam romped with Eve in a natural paradise until lured by Satan to bite the forbidden apple.

Almost every family of fruit tree is represented in the region, from pear to fig. Even the apple—Southern crabapple to be exact—can be found in hollows and deep ravines, along the shores of gold-tinted creeks. Only don't try eating this fruit straight from the branch. Its bitterness will long linger on the palate, and pucker the lips.

The late E.E. Calloway, former minister, NAACP lawyer and one-time Republican nominee for governor from nearby Bristol, maintained that the Apalachicola bluffs and ravines match the biblical description of Eden. Geographically, it lies along the Apalachicola River, a natural waterway formed by four other rivers. Calloway asserted that the original names of the rivers and land were transposed to western Asia and Africa after the Flood and that "those names have had more to do with the assumption that the Garden of Eden was in western Asia than everything else."

On my visits to "Eden", I am always astounded by the abrupt change in scenery and topography. Miles of rolling pine farms, where planted sand pines grow in monotonous rows, give way to expansive arms of moss-bearded live oaks. I drive around a bend and sharply descend, experiencing a rare if not imagined taste of Florida mountain driving.

At road's end, a reconstructed antebellum plantation house right out of *Gone with the Wind* stands atop a tall bluff overlooking the wide Apalachicola River. Touring the structure, I often marvel at the rich river history depicted by drawings and photographs—Indian renegades, riverboat pirates, "Mississippi" gamblers, paddlewheelers and Civil War.

    The house was initially built across the river at Ocheesee Landing by Jason Gregory in 1849 four years after Florida's statehood. Brick pillars kept the house out of reach of flood waters. Gregory soon established the largest plantation spread in the region with vast fields, warehouses, a cotton gin and a steamboat landing—a rising symbol of aristocracy. Then came the Civil War and it ruined him; he moved to Alachua County. The house fell into disrepair, Gregory died of yellow fever, but Gregory's daughter, Chaffa, eventually moved back in 1900 and restored the house. She married a mixed-blood Indian but the marriage was short-lived because he was murdered by river pirates with a hatchet blow to the head. The house was abandoned again and the surviving timbers and boards were eventually ferried plank by plank to the newly formed Torreya State Park in the mid-1930s, reassembled by the Civilian Conservation Corps. The project took three years. Even the original wood pegs that were used instead of nails were painstakingly reinserted.

    As morning sun cast long shadows on antebellum furniture, the mansion itself seems ghost-like, a storehouse of memories and tales of a faded era. Other signs of the plantation days have been reclaimed by nature. Decades before, one could have seen cotton and tobacco fields along with steamships and a loading dock from the bluff. During the "great trading era" from 1840 until 1910, more than 200 steamboats carried goods and passengers up and down the Apalachicola River. Now, only an occasional motorboat interrupts one's reverie. The riverbanks are wild again; trees stretch as far as one can see, and kayakers and canoeists have discovered this treasure, hearkening back to pre-industrial days.

An entirely different view would have greeted onlookers if the Army Corps of Engineers had had their way in the 1970s. A dam fourteen miles to the south would have flooded twenty-seven river miles, altering the floodplain's natural fluctuations and holding back water during dry months in order for barges to have year-round shipping. Most biologists agreed that reduced river flows would have threatened Apalachicola Bay's multi-million dollar seafood industry. Residents up and down the river opposed the dam. After years of hearings and impact statements, the Corps was finally sent packing. The 107-mile Apalachicola remains one of the largest free-flowing rivers of its size in the United States. Current battles center on existing and projected upstream water withdrawals in Alabama and Georgia, but the dam proposal has yet to reemerge.

More than fifteen miles of hiking trails wind along the Apalachicola River and interior ravines in the park, and newly acquired adjacent lands will likely open up new hiking opportunities. The terrain is surprisingly steep and the day hiker has the choice of taking one of two seven-mile loop trails; both if one seeks a strenuous challenge. Three backcountry campsites have been strategically placed for those seeking to stretch out the experience.

I often hike the river loop. I usually begin at the mansion and soon descend the bluff past sites of Civil War battery placements once geared for shooting Union boats. The guns never saw action. The raptor's view of this valley remained peaceful during the war years.

Moving onward, the terrain becomes steep. Large roots finger over the trail, having created earthen steps in angled hillsides. Broad-headed skinks scurry through brown leaf mold and, if it is spring, over fallen blossoms of dogwood and flame azalea. Large white atamasco lilies and trillium flowers sometimes fringe the trail along with bright red carpets of Indian pink. Needle palm, river cane and the taller oak leaf hydrangea dominate the larger understory of flora. Overhead, huge magnolia, beech, white oak and sweetgum trees form lush, shaded canopies.

Rare Torreya tree in Torreya State Park.

Deep in the ravines, amid tiny fingerlings of cascading water, is where I usually find the Torreya tree, otherwise known as "stinking cedar." Its dark green, waxy needles fan symmetrically on either side of a spindly trunk. "The tree is pyramidal in form, of somber appearance, and appears strangely out of place in this latitude among oaks, beeches, and populars," wrote A.H. Curtis in 1884 in a report to the Commissioner of Agriculture. "No doubt the *Torreya* is a relic of a past epoch, when it may have had a wide range at the time when the elephant and mastodon were denizens of this country."

E.E. Calloway maintained that the torreya was the famous gopherwood that built the ark. The wood's resin has a pungent odor, thus the "stinking cedar" moniker, something Noah would surely have found repulsive when mixed with other smells in an animal-packed ark. Torreya, along with the similar looking Florida Yew, grows naturally nowhere else in the world. Once cut for fence posts, a fungal blight now strikes down each torreya tree before they reach maturity, threatening this rare species with extinction.

Torreya Park is where I often stretch my botanical knowledge. If this area is not the biblical Eden, then it surely is a botanical one. There is Appalachian mountain laurel, Carolina poplar, ashe magnolia, bloodroot and downy rattlesnake plantain, all species more commonly found in Southern Appalachia. Several seed varieties may have floated down the Apalachicola, the river being the only Florida watercourse with mountain origins.

Another theory stipulates that northern plants and animals once dominated north Florida during the ice ages. When glaciers retreated and warmer species took over, these northern species found refuge in the cool ravines that were carved into the bluffs. In all, twenty-two northern plant species now thrive in the Apalachicola bluff area along with northern species of spiders, insects, snakes and salamanders. Even scientists not known for exaggeration will heap praise on Torreya's wooded environs.

"The Apalachicola ravines area is believed to have the highest diversity of plants and animals of any comparably sized area on the southeastern coastal plain, and the greatest number of endangered and threatened plant species in Florida," wrote University of Florida Zoologist Dr. John Kaufman in the early 1980s. "This area may represent the center of evolution for the Gulf coastal plain." That's a big claim, but Kaufman supports his statement by describing how the area derives its unusually rich flora and fauna from four major areas of endemism: the Appalachian Mountains and Piedmont to the north, the Florida peninsula to the south, the Atlantic coastal plain to the east, and the Gulf coastal plain. Not surprisingly, in the year 2000, the Nature Conservancy highlighted the Apalachicola River bluffs and ravines as a major reason north Florida was selected as one of six regions in the United States having the highest levels of biodiversity.

In one spot along the trail, a stone bridge arches over a rushing stream, another remnant of the CCC. Side trails lead to a palmetto-fringed waterfall, beaver dams, and more unique flora.

I once forsook the marked path to follow a stream to its origin—a unique three-sided canyon known as a steephead. A clear cool seepage spring emerged from sand at the base. In lush ravines like these, the rare Apalachicola dusky salamander can be found along with the equally rare goldstripe darter fish. But I was more interested in cooling my feet and gazing upon a majestic canopy of American beech, tulip poplar and southern magnolia. There was also basswood and hornbeam, hackberry and ironwood. The red buckeye and aromatic Florida star anise dominated the understory. Clusters of tiny white sparkleberry blossoms hung like frozen dewdrops.

    Since it was mid-spring in this Eden-like environment, mosquitoes were sparse. The main crop was due in a couple of weeks. Ticks, however, had their own time frame. I had to constantly check arms and legs, especially for newly-hatched "seed ticks" which compensate for their lack of size by attacking in sheer numbers. Add chiggers, biting flies, gnats, no-see-ums and hot, humid temperatures later in the year, and you've got the makings of a place quite opposite of Eden.

    Eden is best with a slight nip in the air, when all-encompassing breezes sweep across the bluffs as if sent by gods.

    Some day, when I am gray-haired and in the autumn of life, I will visit Torreya to hike the same trails and touch the same trees of my youth. I will smell flowers of a new spring, sense the alpha and omega of my bodily existence, and grasp the unceasing life force. Isn't that what an Eden is for—a barometer of existence, a place for searching and finding, a place to jump off from?

    Torreya is Eden. It is completely unique, and yet, there are a thousand more like it in Florida, in forests and rivers, coastlines and swamps. It is found in small nooks of greenery, whether a city park or backyard, porch or rooftop garden. It is anywhere people have yearned for the natural, and have found it. It is, simply, Eden.

If You Go

Besides hiking, Torreya State Park has a full-service campground on a high bluff overlooking the river along with three remote hike-in campsites and two youth group camping areas. Ranger-guided tours of the Gregory Mansion are held at 10:00 a.m. on weekdays and at 10, 2, and 4 on weekends and holidays. For more information, log onto http://www.floridastateparks.org/torreya/default.cfm.

For more good hiking in the region, travel a few miles south of Torreya State Park to the trailhead for the Garden of Eden Trail just north of Bristol along Highway 12. This is part of the Nature Conservancy's 6,295-acre Apalachicola Bluff and Ravines Preserve. The 3.7 mile loop trail is one of the most difficult—and scenic—day hikes in Florida, with the highlight being a spectacular vista of the Apalachicola River and floodplain from atop Alum Bluff, the largest natural geologic exposure in Florida. For more information, log onto http://www.nature.org/ourinitiatives/regions/northamerica/unitedstates/florida/apalachicola-bluffs-and-ravines-preserve.xml. Allow three to four hours to complete the trail, and bring a camera! And note that the natural looking and vibrant longleaf pine sandhill forests are a result of more than a quarter century of restoration efforts by the Conservancy. Endangered species such as indigo snakes are being reintroduced to the property.

25
The Great Bradwell Bay Swamp Hike

"At this point, the newcomer to Bradwell Bay is likely to become slightly drunk. The tall trees beckon on every side. Their crowns, high in the heavens, shade the swamp from which they rise, keeping the understory thinned out enough to lure the unwary ever farther from the last flag, deep into the silence and majesty of the great swamp."
>   Betty M. Watts, *The Watery Wilderness of Apalach, Florida,* 1975

Viewing the world record trees in north Florida's 24,600-acre Bradwell Bay Wilderness Area takes some grit and determination. First, you have to drive 30 miles southwest of Tallahassee through the massive Apalachicola National Forest. Once parked at one of four trailheads for the Florida Trail, you walk—or wade—at least three miles to the "big tree area." The old-growth tupelo gum trees are well hidden in a deep swamp amid knee-deep water and a tangle of vines and undergrowth.

I like to hike in from the west side along the unpaved Forest Road 314 because it's the shortest distance to the big trees and the trail is usually well maintained. Still, after only a quarter mile, a span of ankle-deep water about a hundred yards long must be traversed through a strand of water-loving titi trees. I call it the "weeding out" area. Since it's usually winter when I explore the swamp, and temperatures have often dipped below freezing the night before, most newcomers who are with me have a "what have I got myself into" look on their face once the shockingly cold water inundates socks and shoes.

"It's not so bad once your feet get numb," I tell them. I sometimes wear waterproof socks, but that only tempers the initial shock. There's a reason why *Backpacker* Magazine called this one of the ten toughest hikes in the United States.

If the water in this first wet stretch is knee-deep or higher due to a major rain event such as a tropical storm, then it's time to turn around. That means that the water level in the big swamp might be waist deep or chest deep and possibly too dangerous for hiking. And if it's any season except winter, the mosquitoes can seem life threatening.

For the next two-and-a-half miles after this first wet stretch, the hike is primarily in open pine woods on an abandoned tram rail line. Most of Bradwell Bay was logged in the early twentieth century, but the tramways stopped at the big swamp. It was just too impenetrable. The large grove of virgin trees were first protected in 1963 when it was designated a scenic area by the United State Forest Service. In 1975, Congress included the entire roadless area into the national wilderness preservation system. Only foot travel is allowed and Florida Trail crews can only use non-mechanized hand tools to maintain the trail—no chainsaws, bush hogs or weed whackers.

Wildfires erupt on occasion in Bradwell Bay, often burning several thousand acres. The last fire was in 2004. But the flames usually die out in the shaded big tree area, even if it is bone dry due to prolonged drought. The surrounding piney woods and titi strands recover quickly to where only bleached and blackened pine snags serve as reminders of past infernos. This natural process is nature's way of cleaning the forest of excess debris and allowing new growth to sprout from the forest floor. It makes for a lot of extra work for trail crews, however. "It seems that every old dead tree falls right across the trail," complained one volunteer.

From the piney woods, the trail makes an obvious change once in the heart of the swamp. Light is significantly diminished as every living plant and tree seems to be fighting for available sunlight. The water is deeper, the ground spongy from sphagnum moss and thick layers of leaves and pine needles. The air feels fresh and moist, and it's also sweet smelling, partly from the presence of numerous red bay trees, the aromatic leaves of which can be used as seasoning like the California bay.

Spans of tannin-tinted water are not as shallow as they first appear, and the deepest holes are often in the trail itself, perhaps wallowed out by hikers who have struggled through. Several hikers have lost shoes and boots in the sucking mud. A walking staff helps with stability but only if it's arm-thick. A thin stick or pole simply sinks down into the almost quicksand-like muck.

To see the largest tupelo gum trees, of which Bradwell Bay boasts two national co-champions, one must

The bulbous base of a huge tupelo gum in Bradwell Bay.

veer north of the trail and wander about a quarter mile. A compass and GPS unit are a must. This swamp was named for a 19th century hunter who became lost in the swamp and took several days to find his way out. Even in winter, vines can be entangling and visibility is diminished by the thickness of the trees and plant growth. The reward, however, is to admire and touch trees that are centuries old. Many are hollow, but still living, their bases bulbous and full of character. If ever there were an ideal home for gnomes, this would be it.

Several wildlife species such as deer and coyote find the remote Bradwell Bay to their liking. Their narrow trails are everywhere. I once followed tracks of a large black bear for several miles through the swamp and found a territorial marker tree that had been slashed by large claws. It only confirmed to me that the great swamp is more suited to infrequent human visitors who take only photographs and leave an occasional shoe stuck in the mud.

If You Go

Cooler months are ideal times to trek into Bradwell Bay when reptilian life forms and bugs are less prevalent, but bear in mind that water from a large rain event can sit in the large swamp bowl for several weeks. To check on conditions, call the U.S. Forest Service at (850) 926-3561 during weekdays. Trail maps can be obtained from the Florida Trail Association, http://www.floridatrail.org/. Due to the challenging nature of the hike, it is best not to venture into the swamp alone. The Apalachee chapter of the Florida Trail Association organizes an annual winter trek into the swamp, so this is ideal for an initial journey.

Hunting is allowed in Bradwell Bay, but no vehicles are allowed.

26
The Aucilla Wilds

"Sinks, or sink holes, such as the country to the east of this abounds in, are common to all limestone formations. They are sudden and sometimes very deep depressions or breaks in the surface of the ground, caused by the wearing away of the limestone beneath it by underground currents or rivers. In most of these holes standing water or great depth is found, and sometimes swiftly running water. I know several men who have on their places what they call 'natural wells,' or small, deep holes in the ground, at the bottom of which flow streams of water. Many of these sinks are very dangerous, as they open so abruptly that a person might walk into one of them on a dark night before he was aware of its presence. Several people who have mysteriously disappeared in this country are supposed to have lost their lives in that way."
      Kirk Munroe, *Wakulla,* 1885

Every time I approach the great hardwood bottomlands of the Aucilla River along Highway 98 in North Florida, I feel engulfed by a sense of wildness. The green swath is unbroken for several miles, serving as a refuge for black bear, turkey, deer and other wildlife. And it draws people who seek untrammeled places.

The most unique part of this area lies above 98, between the lower and middle portions of the Aucilla River, much of which lies within the protected reaches of the 47,532-acre Aucilla Wildlife Management Area. Known as the Aucilla sinks, here is where the Aucilla River dips underground for several miles and emerges for short stretches in a series of dark sinks and shelf caves. It's as if the river is playing a type of peek-a-boo with the surface. Roots of cypress and other trees knot around moss-covered limestone boulders and steep banks. Everything on the surface finds reflection on the still surface of tannin waters.

Many of the sinks have names: Chocolate, New, Mosquito Slap, Hurry Up, Kitchen, Long Suffering, Watts, Frink, Sunshine, Long, Break-down, Roadside, Overflow, and Silver Blaze Tree. And, like in Kirk Munroe's early description, most of the sinks have a current. In his fictional young adult book, a boy falls into one of the sinks at night and is carried underground, only managing to survive by breathing air pockets at the top of the caves. Eventually, he pops up in someone's natural well.

> He found that he could touch bottom most of the time, though every now and then he had to swim

for greater or less distances, but he was always carried swiftly onward. He tried to keep his hands extended in front of him as much as possible, to protect himself from projecting rocks, but several times his head and shoulders struck heavily against them.

Once, for quite a distance, the roof was so low that there was barely room for his head between it and the water. A few inches lower would have drowned him, but it got higher again, and he went on.

Suddenly the air seemed purer and cooler, and the current was not so strong. Mark looked up and saw a star—yes, actually a star—twinkling down at him like a beacon light. He was in water up to his shoulders, but the current was not strong; he could maintain his footing and hold himself where he was.

The best way to see the Aucilla sinks is to hike a three-mile section of the 1300-mile Florida Trail. The orange-blazed footpath skirts several of the sinks, and wooden foot-bridges span low areas. Only make sure you go in the daytime.

On the Aucilla River, above the sinks area, a challenging stretch of water draws paddlers. Known as the "Big Rapid," one of only a handful of whitewater shoals in Florida, the eight to 10 foot drop over 30 yards can provide a rush of adrenalin for even the stoutest paddler. Limestone boulders frame a rushing stream that seems more reminiscent of Appalachian waterways.

The Florida Trail also skirts this section of the Aucilla River before veering east towards the Suwannee. Winding tannin water flows beneath arching live oaks, river birch and cypress. Designated campsites along secluded bends ensure that hikers will have the scenic river all to themselves.

Wildlife can often be spotted by the quiet traveler. I once paddled the middle Aucilla and paused upon hearing a loud continuous cracking sound. It took me a couple of minutes to pick out a sleek river otter camouflaged amid black limestone. It was breaking open the shell of a Suwannee cooter.

On another occasion, while fishing for bream along the Aucilla Sinks with my father, we startled a five-foot diamondback rattlesnake. It had been lying quietly beneath a palmetto bush. The snake rattled but never coiled and slowly crawled away when we retreated.

Different times of year can lure different wildlife. Soaring swallow-tailed kites are often seen during spring and summer, while bald eagles can be spotted in winter. Deer, turkey and black bear find the hardwood hammocks of the Aucilla region to their liking. Bream and catfish are often caught in the sinks and river. Alligators can be seen on most sunny days.

Plants have their seasons, too. Purple violets blanket the forest floor in early spring. Blue and purple flag irises can be found in wet areas along with brilliant red cardinal flowers and white atamasco lilies. Springtime brings an array of colors to the river trees as they leaf out in various shades of bright green, along with the reds of swamp maple and redbud. Fall along the Aucilla River and Sinks can remind visitors of northern states as hardwoods trees are resplendent in yellow and orange leaves, and cypress needles turn gold.

Whatever season or mode of travel you choose, a visit to the Aucilla River and sinks is an opportunity to touch wild Florida at its best.

If You Go

While hiking is ideal in the cooler months, canoeing and kayaking on the Aucilla River can be an enjoyable year-round pursuit as long as water levels are sufficient. When too low, strainers and exposed limestone shoals will require paddlers to drag boats or portage around the obstacles. When too high, the river can dump paddlers into overhanging branches. The best way to determine flow is to access satellite-linked river gauges that are found on the Suwannee River Water Management District Website:

http://www.srwmd.state.fl.us/realtimeriverlevels/realtimeriverlevels.asp. Ideal water levels for paddling below Highway 27 are between 48 and 50 feet at the Lamont gauge. The river above Highway 27 can have numerous obstructions.

To learn more about hiking along the Aucilla, contact the Florida Trail Association: http://www.floridatrail.org. The area is also open for hunting and fishing. Hunters, hikers and bank fishermen should wear bright orange clothing during hunting seasons. To learn more about the Aucilla Wildlife Management Area and recreation opportunities, log onto http://myfwc.com/recreation/aucilla/recreation.asp. To learn more about paddling the Aucilla River, log onto www.dep.state.fl.us/gwt/guide/designated_paddle/**Aucilla_guide.pdf**.

27
Where Wilderness Takes Over

Florida is unkind to vestiges of human history. Water, insects, heat, fire, storms and a long growing season often obliterate signs of the past in a relatively short period of time. So it didn't surprise me that the old rail bed of the Loping Gopher—the Live Oak, Perry and Gulf Railroad (LOP&G)—was overgrown with sable palms and native cane, and most of the original swamp bridges were gone.

      To reach the rail bed, I had hiked along the Florida Trail south of Highway 98 near the Aucilla River through the Aucilla Wildlife Management Area in Florida's Big Bend. After entering the St. Marks National Wildlife Refuge, I headed east along the abandoned East-West rail tram, while the Florida Trail veered west. I'm not sure what I was searching for in the thick tangle of trees and vines. Perhaps I merely wanted to touch a bit of Florida history.

"The Lopin' Gopher (LOP&G) was an important rail line during the days of the big sawmills," wrote R.C. Balfour III, author of *In Search of the Aucilla*. "It linked the mill towns and centers together and joined the Seaboard Air Line Railroad at Live Oak to complete the connection to Jacksonville, Florida. At the point where it crossed the Aucilla, the Fish House was built on the side of the trestle, giving commercial fishermen a fast and reliable delivery system to towns and cities."

The "Lopin' Gopher" rail line today through the Aucilla bottomlands.

Early locomotives were known as 'cabbage heads.' They burned lightered pine, while the cabbage stacks swirled sparks until they cooled, preventing forest fires. One early LOP&G excursion train seated about eighty passengers and reached speeds of almost seventy miles per hour, but lumber was the main commodity for the Loping Gopher. Historians suggest that the train carried more lumber related traffic than any other short line railroad in Florida.

Today, the Loping Gopher line is no longer a place for man. Wilderness has reasserted itself, and the human is now an infrequent visitor who must move at a gopher tortoise pace. Not surprisingly, this area known as the Aucilla bottomlands was designated a federal wilderness area in the early 1970s, soon after the wilderness act was passed by congress. It isn't virgin land. Loggers cut the original trees and built the raised tram, but the bottomlands are wild again, and if left undisturbed the swamp forest will slowly reclaim its old-growth glory.

I found a long beam of rusted metal, no doubt part of the old rail line or logging operations. A stack of moss-covered logs lay nearby, cypress that had been cut but never used. The roar of steam engines and grunting men were no more. Only the distant drone of an airplane.

Florida has hundreds of lost towns and their associated roads and rail lines. They originally sprung up to cut trees, tap pines for turpentine, mine phosphate, net fish, or entice people to soak in mineral springs. Most are gone, reclaimed by nature or paved over to make new dwellings or roads. Along the coast, many defunct hamlets and fish houses are sinking beneath ocean waters as sea level rises.

Men and women worked long hard hours in those early Florida endeavors, often risking life and limb. Little room was left for pencil pushers. To make a living then, especially in rural Florida, one had to exploit the natural resources, whether plant, animal or mineral. Conservation was largely an abstract concept.

In another part of the St. Marks Refuge, my wife and I once hiked to the place where Port Leon once existed along the St. Marks River. There was nothing left to see. There were a few foundation pilings just off the trail, but those were from an early refuge headquarters, not Port Leon. That's the remarkable thing about this former town of 450 along the lower St. Marks River. You can hike or bike there, heading west about three-and-a-half miles from the St. Marks Refuge Visitor's Center on an unpaved refuge road or the Florida Trail. When you near the St. Marks River, there it is, or was, in a spacious pine and live oak forest—a once bustling port town that was connected to St. Marks and Tallahassee by an infamous mule-drawn railroad.

"The railroad is certainly the worst that has been built in the entire world," wrote French traveler Count de Castelnau in 1838. "The road, however, is useful, for without its help it would be almost impossible to take a heavy load of cotton across the sand that covers the country to the south, into which the horses sink at every step. They have tried several times to put a locomotive on this railroad, but its construction is so poor that the plan has been admitted to be impossible. ... Moreover, instead of being astonished at the bad construction of this railroad, one is inclined on the other hand to admire the bold thought that inspired a project of such a sort in a country inhabited by hostile savages and through almost impassible forests, which, so few years ago were not even explored by the whites."

From the Port Leon town site, you can walk on an old tram to the river's edge and enjoy a spacious view of water and marsh, and imagine sailing ships being loaded with cotton from North Florida and South Georgia plantations bound for the United States East Coast. Only a few anglers and paddlers move on the river now, along with manatees, dolphins, and schools of fish.

It's almost scary how Mother Nature can erase signs of man, especially near the coast. In the case of Port Leon, two major calamities occurred in less than a decade. Established in 1837, the town quickly grew based on a gross inaccuracy. According to a refuge brochure, advertisements stated that Port Leon was "handsomely located on the most elevated site on the bay… beyond the influence of the highest tides."

At its peak, the town boasted a hotel, two taverns, stores, a post office, newspaper, and warehouses, but then a three-month yellow fever epidemic struck, brought by a Key West boat passenger. Residents fled or succumbed to the disease, and the town's population was cut to less than half.

As the town slowly recovered, Port Leon was named the Wakulla County seat when the county was formed in March of 1843. But six months later, disaster struck again in the form of a hurricane. While only one resident died, the ten-foot storm surge devastated the town and severely damaged nearby St. Marks. The townspeople decided to abandon all hope of rebuilding Port Leon and move five miles upriver near a sulphur spring. This is how the town of Newport came into being, a town that still stands, albeit a shadow of its former self.

Port Leon now belongs to the alligators, deer and other critters; not a soul lives there.

On another occasion, I pushed through a jungle of growth to see the foundations of Centralia, an early logging town of more than 1,500 near Weeki Wachee that is now part of the Chassahowitzka Wildlife Management Area. "The huge mill operated from 1910 to 1921 and then closed after exhausting the supply of local cypress timber," wrote James R. Warnke in *Ghost Towns of Florida*. "At that time a passenger train made a daily round trip to Tampa along with heavy trainloads of lumber for the waiting boats in Tampa Bay. By 1930, most of the buildings had been torn down or destroyed by fire."

I gazed in awe at what little remained of Centralia, and how vines, moss and trees gave concrete footers the appearance of Mayan ruins. So much can change after only eight or nine decades. Not surprisingly, the Florida wild has virtually obscured untold number of Native American villages that existed for hundreds and thousands of years. A mound here, a midden there, a piece of pottery or chert, that's about it. But I enjoy the feeling of standing where humans once carried on busy lives. Echoes of their passing still resound through the land. The ghosts of those long ago towns and villages remind me that physical life is finite.

When barely in my twenties, a friend told me about a huge Indian temple mound along the Apalachicola River. When I showed interest, he offered to take me there.

It wasn't an easy task. We drove down an unpaved floodplain road until one of many huge holes threatened to swallow a tire or front end. Then, on foot, we worked our way along the riverbank, climbing over tree roots and dodging mud until he said it was time to move inland. We walked through a hardwood forest where dappled sunlight danced on bright green leaves. Woodpeckers darted across the woody path—swift wings—flashes of black, white and red. We pushed through sticky spider webs. Due to recent rains, the leaf-littered ground was spongy, the air sweet smelling.

Abruptly, it seemed, because of the dense woods, we came upon the massive three-story temple mound, its surface covered in old-growth trees and arm-thick grape vines. A small pond lay beside it, thickly bordered by vines and shrubs. This was where early Native Americans scooped up dirt to build the mound, basketful by basketful. "Let's climb it," my friend suggested.

I wanted to climb the mound, to look out over the valley like early priests from their wood and palm-thatched huts, but I couldn't compel my legs to move very fast. It was like a dream where you want to run, but just can't. About halfway up, I stopped while my friend continued on. I felt I was intruding. For the valley's ancient people, this was a sacred place, an altar that had seemed to merge the thoughts and prayerful ritual of a faded civilization with the wildness of a North Florida river valley.

While I waited for my friend, it was easy to look out over the thick grove of trees and envision the broad village that once existed. Clusters of huts and racks of drying meat were situated around a central square. Smoke from cook fires hovered like fog and bare-breasted women pounded corn into meal with large wood mortars and pestles. Children ran about playfully with toy bows, arrows and spears while dust-covered dogs barked excitedly, running after them. In the distance were great fields of corn, beans and squash, food to feed thousands.

On the river itself, dugout canoes moved about as people fished or embarked on trade journeys—south to the sea, north to the mountains. The river was a canoe path to many places.

From the forest edge, men returned with freshly killed wild turkey, eastern bison and deer. The men's bodies nearly matched the color of clay and earth. Their faces bore the satisfied countenances of a successful hunt.

For a few moments, I touched the past and began to ponder my own mortality, and that of our current culture. Civilizations and towns have risen and fallen over millennia. People have peeled back the skin of Mother Earth to work the land and build their homes, only to have their works one day be covered again by the wild green veneer of life. Most likely, many of our modern towns will fare no differently. And after Florida's wet, corrosive environment performs its disappearing act on our creations, how will future generations interpret the last remnants of our passing?

Take a walk along the old Loping Gopher rail line or view some other nearly forgotten vestige of civilization from a period not so long ago, and see for yourself.

If You Go

The best way to reach the old Loping Gopher rail line or the Port Leon site is by way of the Florida National Scenic Trail. To learn more, log onto to the website of the Apalachee Chapter of the Florida Trail Association:

http://apalachee.floridatrail.org . Maps are available for downloading from the Trails and Hiking section.

28
Racing Mosquitoes at Wakulla State Forest

The Wakulla State Forest. I had passed the sign dozens of times along Highway 267 near the entrance of Wakulla Springs State Park and had never stopped. Most of the 4,219-acre tract was acquired by the state from the St. Joe Corporation between 2001 and 2003, mainly as a protective buffer for below-ground conduits that lead to Wakulla Springs.

On a late summer afternoon after a thunderstorm subsided, I finally decided to check out one of our newest state forests. I pulled into the gravel parking lot and found it empty. My first thought was, "cool, I have the place all to myself!" My second thought was, "why do I have the place all to myself?"

I paid my $2 fee at an iron ranger, glanced at a trail map, and took off riding my mountain bike down Double Springs Road. The road, closed to vehicles, was open and dry, making for easy riding. If the entire 4.5 mile Double Springs Loop Trail was like this, I thought about riding it twice. A spotted fawn jumped out in front of me and bounded away. That was an unexpected surprise. And I spotted bobwhite quail, too.

Double Springs was my first stop and I stopped to admire the reflections and wilderness character of this watery oasis. Not surprisingly, the place had a healthy population of mosquitoes. The swamp angels harassed me until I took off riding again down the road. That's one advantage of a mountain bike—you can out-run most any flying insect.

Wet section of trail in the Wakulla State Forest.

I became a little confused as to where the Double Springs Loop continued to my left since Double Springs Road eventually veered right and off the map. So, I studied my trail map, backtracked, and decided to take another forest road that met up with the loop trail—Forest Road 211. That was a huge mistake. I barely made it through the first dump truck-sized puddle, but I bogged down in the next and fell over in knee-deep water. That's when I realized you can't outrun mosquitoes while trying to ride through water. Muddy and wet, I pushed onward through more puddles and waist-high ragweed. In the fall, this would be a hayfever sufferer's gauntlet!

Not all outdoor adventures are worthy of glowing accounts, but I did begin to laugh aloud at my predicament. I had reached the point of no return, meaning it was just as far to go back as it was to go forward.

I finally re-connected with the loop trail and found it to be just as wet and nearly as overgrown. My conclusion upon reaching the parking lot: the Wakulla State Forest is best done in cool, dry weather. And except for the scenic swamps, the uplands are a work-in-progress as the Florida Forest Service has begun the long process of converting a former slash pine plantation to a more natural pine forest. It will be interesting to follow the restoration progress—in the winter months!

If You Go

For more information about the Wakulla State Forest, log onto http://www.floridaforestservice.com/state_forests/wakulla.html.

29
Restoration Beginnings at St. Sebastian

"Putting a landscape together is a lot like doing a big jigsaw puzzle. Working a jigsaw puzzle, I start with the straight-edged pieces, so I get a frame first. For a landscape, you can't draw a big rectangle on a map and start filling it in. Restoration is more arbitrary. You start with what wild land you have. Then you look for spare pieces scattered about that match what you already have. If one fits, you plug it in, and then find another with the same thread of stream, and another. ... Until you begin to see the shapes of the missing pieces, and you search for those shapes. Piece by piece, the puzzle is assembled, reassembled, until it forms a picture. ... The picture grows more beautiful."

> Janisse Ray, *Pinhook: Finding Wholeness in a Fragmented Land*

Many central and south Florida lands purchased for conservation were once large ranches, ranches with man-made ditches and significant areas of improved pasture that challenge land managers who seek a more natural ecosystem. A prime example of efforts to restore former pastureland is at the 22,000-acre St. Sebastian River Preserve State Park near the town of Sebastian, in southeast Florida. On a visit a few years ago, I sought to glimpse the tools land managers utilize to restore and manage public lands.

Upon arriving, I was confronted by two Florida sandhill cranes, almost four feet tall, standing defiantly in the center of the unpaved entrance road like trained sentinels. They peered at my stopped car, then proceeded to feed on grasshoppers, unmoved. As I tried to pass around them, the birds unleashed a bone-chilling cry—a cross between a garbled laugh and an underwater scream. So much for my hoped for quiet arrival. My presence was now known to every critter within honking distance.

The state threatened Florida sandhill crane is one of several state or federally protected wildlife species found on the sanctuary. Established in 1995 with funds from Florida's Preservation 2000 and Save our Rivers programs, the park was originally set up as an upland buffer preserve for the St. Sebastian River, which feeds into the Indian River Lagoon. It later became a state park.

Twenty-four different habitat types are found here, from oak scrub to wet prairie, including the increasingly rare longleaf pine ecosystem. Longleaf pine habitat once covered seventy to eighty million acres of the southeastern United States; today only a small fraction remains, mostly on public lands. The Sebastian preserve park boasts the largest chunk of longleaf habitat in southeast Florida, and this is the most southern range of the species. Credit that to previous owners who left large areas relatively undisturbed for free-range cattle.

Within minutes of walking through one of the park's longleaf tracts, I scared up a deer, then a wild turkey. A covey of quail took off, too. I began feeling like Attila the Hun romping through the forest. Then a large gopher tortoise came racing down the sand path towards me. "Racing" may sound like an odd term to describe a tortoise, but gopher tortoises are faster than you might think. Those legs are strong from digging burrows anywhere from twelve to forty-eight feet in length and six to nine feet deep. As it drew close, I momentarily wondered if it was an emissary for the sentinel cranes until I saw its burrow directly to my left. I stepped aside, and he disappeared down the dark tunnel.

Gopher tortoises are considered a keystone species in longleaf habitat. Over one hundred different species of animals and insects, including a variety of snakes, frogs, mice and beetles, are known to seek refuge in gopher burrows, including endangered indigo snakes. For animals that can neither fly, climb, nor sprint, burrows provide protection from severe weather, predators and fire.

Fire is a catalyst in longleaf habitat. Plants and trees depend on it to open up soil for seed germination, and many wildlife species such as gopher tortoises rely on succulent grasses and legumes available only in an open forest environment with plenty of sunlight. In one area of the park, where a lightning fire had recently burned several hundred acres, the understory of grasses and palmetto displayed bright green new growth reminiscent of early spring, even though it was late summer.

There was little evidence of plants having been killed by the fire; roots were still alive and most had re-sprouted. Even foot-tall longleaf pines, still in the "grass stage" because they resemble large clumps of grass, stood undamaged by the flames. During fire, burning green needles create a type of moisture shield for the plant's terminal bud. Generally, only a very hot fire, one fueled by drought and a heavy build-up of fallen leaves and pine needles, will kill a longleaf pine.

In pre-settlement times, lightning fires spread over great expanses of upland forests, sometimes for weeks, until reaching a river or large wetlands. In the pine flatwoods, these low-intensity fires would occur every one to eight years; other types of ecosystems would burn at different intervals. But with human development, agriculture and fire suppression, natural environments and fire cycles became fragmented. Uplands managers, such as those at the park, must carefully ignite periodic prescribed fire to mimic natural fire regimes, that is, unless lightning saves them the trouble.

Continuing my walk through a slightly different habitat type, one that contained several small oak trees and thick shrubs, a blue and gray Florida scrub-jay flitted into my path, grabbed an insect, and flew back into the brush. The tract harbors more than 40 scrub-jay families, comprising the largest portion of what biologists call the south Brevard-Indian River-St. Lucie metapopulation.

Sunrise on the preserve brings a whole new array of images and animals. Flowers and spider webs stand out, dew-covered and glistening. The air is filled with bird songs that alternate with the throbbing chirps of crickets and katydids as the louder cries of eagles, osprey and sandhill cranes echo across the land. More and more, these sounds of original Florida instill a sense of homecoming.

Red-cockaded woodpecker cavity.

If quietly poised in the right spot at first light, you're rewarded with a glimpse of endangered red-cockaded woodpeckers leaving their cavities in the oldest longleaf pines for a day of foraging. The preserve harbors about a dozen potential breeding groups of the small black and white birds. During the breeding season, the male woodpecker has a small red streak on each side of its black cap known as a cockade, thus its name. This is the only North American woodpecker that drills a cavity in a living tree, and it takes a group of birds months of diligent work to complete the task. Once occupied by a breeding pair, the birds constantly peck around the nest cavity opening and the resulting flow of sap repels climbing predators, such as rat snakes. Biologists have created artificial nest cavities in living pines to jumpstart the process and the birds are responding favorably. Who wouldn't want a free home?

Some of the park's vast tracts of longleaf forests can seem endless when on foot, and they surely must have seemed that way to early pioneers. There were accounts of driving wagons for miles through the park-like forests with no cleared road or path to follow. "A prairie with trees" was how one early visitor described it, although in these Sebastian woods, you'd have to add lots of palmetto to that description.

Besides appreciating what the park is today, it is inspiring to envision what it will be like in the future. Since purchasing the first tract in 1995 and adding another sizeable chunk in 2000, several areas were targeted for restoration, including 2500 acres of improved pastureland.

Longleaf pines have been planted close together in the dense bahia grass in hopes they will eventually shade out grass and open the way for groundcover restoration. Native grasses such as wiregrass, a thick bunchgrass with blades that resemble baling wire, along with an array of ferns and wildflowers would be part of any complete restoration effort, and this would take time and resources to establish on a large scale.

Then park manager Keith Fisher toured me through a pasture where recently-planted longleafs were just popping their bright green heads over the bahia grass. "The state-of-the-art in pasture restoration is not there yet," he said, spreading out one of the young longleafs in his hands to create a fan of needles. "There is some trial and error, so any success you can get is encouraging."

Fisher paused and scanned the field, summing up the long-term vision of any restoration project. "You know, in sixty to eighty years, there could be red-cockaded woodpeckers right here." I could picture Fisher, in his twenties, walking beneath a longleaf canopy as a gray-haired elder.

Besides wildlife benefits, the restored land will improve water filtration to the river, and visitors to the park's southern entrance will be greeted with an aesthetic tree line instead of open pastureland.

The park staff also filled in several miles of ditches to reestablish the natural water connections to the north and south forks of the still largely unspoiled St. Sebastian River. A third fork, Sebastian Creek, was severely altered by an Army Corps of Engineers canal in 1968. Ironically, it is at the canal's water control structure that you'll find the most manatees on a cool winter's day. Sometimes more than a hundred of the endangered sea cows have been seen in a single day. That's because water depth exceeds fourteen feet and is not as affected by cool air.

Other wildlife such as river otters, wood storks, white ibis, great blue herons, limpkins and great egrets can be spotted in the canal and at the many marshes, ponds and wet prairies within the preserve and along the eight miles of Sebastian River frontage. The sandhill cranes prefer shallow freshwater marshes adjacent to upland environments, a mix of habitats commonly found at the preserve.

Appropriately enough, on my last hike through the preserve I found a spot where several old-growth longleafs had formed a natural ring less than a hundred yards from the Sebastian River. Many were bonsai shaped, twisted and bent by coastal storms; one had been "cat-faced" by turpentiners in the '30s or '40s. Long, gray diagonal slash scars completely covered one side of the trunk, yet the tree still appeared vigorous. It was here that I sat and waited out the afternoon's heat. Gentle breezes, spawned by the nearby Atlantic Ocean, soothed my tired body and swayed the shimmering fans of pine needles overhead. I lay back on a bed of fallen needles and closed my eyes.

These tree sentinels witnessed droughts, fires, hurricanes, logging, turpentining and development across the river. They watch over land once revered by Native Americans, long coveted by land speculators, and now appreciated by modern day visitors for what it is and what it yet can be. It stabs at my conscience to think of what has been lost; it heartens me to know that some lands can be restored, that we have the vision and fortitude to say, "Yes, this place is special, let us protect and restore this place."

As Keith Fisher put it to me while standing among the newly planted longleafs: "I was born and raised in Florida. I spent a lot of time in the woods growing up and a lot of those woods aren't there anymore. I want to do what I can to preserve, restore and manage what's left."

Perhaps other animals will find their home again at St. Sebastian—the panther, for one, and the Florida black bear. As sprawl touches more of Florida, we can take heart that some of it can be restored—we can give back to the land—and it has already begun at the St. Sebastian River Preserve State Park. If you visit, just don't expect a quiet greeting from the sandhill cranes at the entrance.

If You Go

The St. Sebastian River Preserve State Park boasts 60 miles of trails for equestrians, hikers, and mountain bikers. The park offers six primitive hike-in tent camping sites, two camping areas for equestrians, and five group sites. One can access the park by canoe or kayak along the St. Sebastian River, but there are no launch facilities in the park. Paddlers generally launch from the Donald MacDonald Park or Dale Wimbrow Park off Roseland Road or at the Indian River County launch north of the intersection of CR 512 and CR 510. The park is one of the top birding locations in the United States.

To access the state park's north entrance from Interstate 95, take exit 73 and drive east on Malabar Road (State Road 514). Turn south onto Babcock Road (County Road 507) and travel 11.5 miles. Turn east onto Buffer Preserve Drive. The south entrance is off Fellsmere Road (CR 512), 1.8 miles east of I-95. To learn more, log onto http://www.floridastateparks.org/stsebastianriver. For camping reservations, call the park during business hours Monday through Friday at 321-953-5005.

30
Fakahatchee Strand: North America's Amazon

"In no other state are there so many plants of strange habits and remarkable characteristics."
    Mary Frances Baker, *Florida Wildflowers,* 1926

When I pushed back the man-sized sword ferns obscuring the trail, I spotted them—fresh panther tracks in black mud. I glanced around, hopeful. Royal palms towered over me. Bromeliad-covered hardwood trees formed a dense canopy, but no panthers. Still, what an incredible home for this endangered mammal—the Fakahatchee Strand, one of the planet's unique habitats.

In short, the Fakahatchee Strand Preserve State Park boasts the largest cypress strand in existence, the orchid and bromeliad capital of North America, the fern capital of Florida, the world's largest stand of royal palms and the only bald cypress/royal palm interface. Plus, its brackish reaches south of the Tamiami Trail contain one of the largest undisturbed mangrove estuaries in North America. Park biologist Mike Owen calls the 77,690-acre Fakahatchee Strand "North America's Amazon."

According to Owen, water carved this shallow limestone valley in southwest Florida over millennia. Deciduous trees emerged—bald cypress, maple, willow, pop ash and an array of others. Their annual shedding of leaves and needles created a spongy layer of earth several feet thick. The earth and peat easily absorbed moisture, nourishing plants during times of drought and creating a line of defense against fire. An immense interlocking canopy of cypress helped to retain humidity, and the slough's deeper channels and lakes helped to shield the forest interior from extreme cold temperatures.

When birds or hurricanes, or both, carried tropical plant seeds from Central and South America and the Caribbean Islands, the plants took root and flourished. The elongated 20-mile strand became a type of tropical greenhouse in a semi-tropical zone. The results were dazzling—44 types of wild orchids, 38 native species of ferns and 14 species of bromeliads. Wildlife found a home, too—panther, Everglades mink, bald eagle, black bear, river otter, deer, wading birds and numerous other species.

"Fakahatchee is important panther habitat," said Mark Lotz, panther biologist for the Florida Fish and

Wildlife Conservation Commission. "It's a link between Big Cypress to the east and Picayune Strand State Forest on the west side, with the panther refuge to the north."

Charles Fergus tracked panthers in the Strand for several years. "I wondered whether Fakahatchee Strand would still be Fakahatchee Strand if a panther were not living in it," he stated in his book, *Swamp Screamer*. Fakahatchee is where the first Florida panthers were found in the early 1970s, when many thought they were extinct in the wild. They've been found there ever since.

Credit for protecting Fakahatchee goes largely to Miami attorney and amateur botanist Mel Finn. Finn made protecting the swamp and personal crusade. He did slide programs, wrote letters and led delegations of political dignitaries into the swamp to keep it from being overlooked as "just another Florida swamp."

"There are sound economic and scientific reasons for protecting Fakahatchee Strand," wrote Finn, "but its beauty alone is reason enough to save it."

Finn's dream was realized three years after his death.

When the state of Florida purchased Fakahatchee in 1974, it was not entirely pristine. The Okaloacoochee Slough to the northeast, Fakahatchee's main feeder stream, had been severed in 1928 and diverted through the Barren River Canal. In 1944 loggers began cutting huge old-growth cypress from the swamp to build hulls for mine sweepers and PT boats. After the war, cypress logging continued as part of the post-war economy. Sawyers made up to $800 a month, good money in those days.

The strand was one of the last old-growth cypress forests in the United States and, not surprisingly, one of the most difficult to log. More than 100 elevated trams were built to haul out the massive trees. Logging was nearly halted in 1948 when Everglades National Park Superintendent Dan Beard toured the Strand and recommended it as a national monument, but he was unsuccessful. When large scale logging ended in 1953, only 215 acres of old-growth bald cypress were spared, trees that can now be seen along the Cypress Bend Boardwalk just off Tamiami Trail.

The logging doomed Fakahatchee's ivory-billed woodpeckers. The last confirmed sighting was in 1938, but "they probably hung on here until the early 1950s," said Owen.

The diminished cypress canopy allowed more sunlight to reach the forest floor. This, combined with decreased water levels caused by canal building, prompted several wildfires to rage through the strand for the first time in recorded history. In 1964 the main railroad bed was turned into a county road, providing easy public access. A decade of plant collection began in which commercial and private collectors took thousands of orchids, bromeliads and other native plants out of Fakahatchee. Numerous small lots were also sold for hunting retreats.

Some of what was lost is irretrievable, but nature does have a way of regenerating herself, sometimes with a little help. In 1989 the main water link to the Okaloacoochee Canal was reconnected. Second-growth cypress have again formed an interlocking canopy in most parts of the strand, and diverse plant life—almost 500 documented species—can still be found. Wildlife, too, are slowly rebounding, minus the ivory-bill. The preserve park is "meant to be large and wild and rustic, with plants and animals coming first," according to Owen.

Hiking through Fakahatchee Strand.

Human visitors are welcome, but there is currently no camping and facilities are minimal. Hiking is generally along one of the old tram rail beds, or one can wade through the swamp to get a glimpse of a native orchid, especially during October, the peak blooming season. The rare ghost orchid, however, blooms in August, when one has to brave ferocious mosquitoes to find it.

Famed black-and-white photographer Clyde Butcher has photographed the blooming ghost orchid on several occasions. On a visit to his Big Cypress studio,

Butcher pointed out differences in the blooms during wet and dry conditions. During a dry period, the bloom is more spread out. Wet conditions cause the orchid to close up slightly, as if to shield itself from rain. "I love the swamp in July and August," he said, "everything stands out."

Regardless of the time of year, whether one is a plant lover, wildlife enthusiast, photographer or just an admirer of natural beauty, a trip to Fakahatchee is a memorable one. The park is a testament to nature's regenerative powers, and to the ability of humans to temper their consumptive habits in order to protect a unique environment.

If You Go

The Fakahatchee Strand Preserve State Park features more than 15 miles of hiking trails (one way) on the many raised railway beds or trams that crisscross the strand, the central one being the East and West Main Tram beginning at Gate 12. Of course, one can also wade through the swamp, but bring along a compass and/or GPS unit. Along the Tamiami Trail (U.S. 41), seven miles west of State Road 29, don't miss the 2,500-foot long boardwalk at Big Cypress Bend adjacent to a small Miccosukee Indian village. To learn more, log onto http://www.floridastateparks.org/fakahatcheestrand/default.cfm. Check the website for guided swamp walks, usually held on the 1st, 2nd and 3rd Saturday from November through April. Call 239-695-1023 for reservations. The 11-mile park road also makes for a scenic drive and the park is also featuring tram tours.

Paddlers often explore the southern reaches of the park, such as the East River, in the mangrove wilderness of the Ten Thousand Islands. Several outer islands are open for camping, although one must obtain a permit if camping to the east in Everglades National Park. A map is located on the state park website under Additional Info.

31
Camping with the He-coon

"The old He-coon walks just before the light of day."
>Lawton Chiles, former United States senator and Florida governor

Like a perceptive country storekeeper, Lawton Chiles determined right away that I wasn't from Florida, and that I hadn't done much hunting. We were sitting around a crackling fire in the Osceola National Forest while husky bear hunters were preparing a carnivorous feast—roasting meat of bear, armadillo and wild hog. A vegetarian's worst nightmare. Chiles, Florida's senior United States senator at the time, eyed my twenty-something face, bushy beard and longish hair. "These people have a small group that hunt only bear," he said. "They have specially trained dogs that won't even bat an eye at a deer."

He studied my reaction; I tried to keep a neutral face, though even then, in 1982, I had never embraced the notion of shooting bears. Something about their high level of intelligence and ability to walk upright. Primitive cousins.

Growing up, I had only one opportunity to hunt. In eighth grade, my friend George invited me on a weekend deer hunt. I was all for it, at first. Then he told me about the ritual that occurs when you kill your first deer. Other hunters wrap you in deer guts. Then, for breakfast, you eat scrambled eggs mixed with deer brain. I was almost relieved when my mother nixed the plan. Thirteen-year-olds toting rifles was not her idea of a safe weekend.

Chiles, born and raised in a hunting family in Lakeland, had hunted with the bear-hunting group before. "We hunted bear for twenty minutes and hunted for the dogs for two days," he joked, tilting his gray cowboy hat back a little. He shoved cold hands into his down hiking vest, gazed into the fire, and his face bore a distinct enigmatic smile. "This is great," he concluded, his blue eyes reflecting firelight, "We've got hunters and anti-hunters here, government people and private citizens, all united for one cause."

The "cause" was survival of the Osceola National Forest—200,000 acres of swamps, pine forests, lakes, rivers and streams just south of the Georgia border that most people only glimpse while whizzing past on Interstate 10. A blur of trees and water. What those highway travelers miss are wild turkey, Florida black bear, endangered red-cockaded woodpeckers, lush ferns, golden clumps of wiregrass and green palmetto fronds that stand against the sun like geometric stained-glass patterns. The forest is part of a wild expanse that stretches all the way to Okefenokee, a system that nourishes the Suwannee and St. Mary's rivers, and also human souls who seek wildness.

Four companies—Monsanto, Pittsburg Midway, Kerr-McGee and Global—applied for leases to strip-mine a third of the forest for phosphate at the behest of then

Secretary of Interior James Watt, perhaps the most infamous person to ever hold that office. Used primarily for fertilizer and animal feed, phosphate was by no means scarce, and its extraction didn't fit in with most folks' idea of public lands stewardship. A loose-knit coalition of diverse forest users formed. I represented the Sierra Club, a California-based conservation organization since 1892 but one that hadn't put down formal roots in Florida until 1970. Being a transplant myself, my marriage to the group fit perfectly.

Signed photo from Lawton Chiles of the campout group. Chiles is kneeling wearing the cowboy hat. I am kneeling, third from left. The inscription reads: "To an Osceola survivor—we made it."

The leader of our "palmetto rebellion" was Chiles, who had risen from virtual obscurity to win a United States senate seat by walking a zigzag route across Florida. He trekked 1000 miles from the Keys to Pensacola and met an estimated 40,000 people along the way. His nickname became "Walkin' Lawton," but during heated political battles, he sometimes referred to himself as the He-coon, a southern reference for the most cunning male raccoon of the pack.

After two terms in the U.S. Senate, Chiles easily won the Florida governorship in 1990. During his 1994 campaign for re-election, however, he found himself trailing opponent Jeb Bush in the polls. When Bush boasted about his lead during a highly publicized debate, Chiles reached back to his roots and rejoined, "The old He-coon walks just before the light of day." His somewhat cryptic, folksy message captured the imagination of Florida voters. Chiles came from behind to win a second term

Chiles had advanced the Osceola fight the Washington way—by filing a bill and joining a lawsuit, but he also sought a more down-to-earth, He-coon approach. And so, at Chiles' behest, a diverse group of folks gathered in the Osceola National Forest for an icy January campout. Reporters and television crews were allowed, but they only stayed during the daytime and filmed us as we hiked the Osceola's trails and pointed out pristine piney woods and swamps that would be leveled by strip-mining. Once temperatures dipped below freezing, with a promise of a record ten-degree night, the media crews wisely left. Those that remained were environmental activists, a few government officials, the bear-hunting group, our bus driver, and Senator Chiles.

Florida icicles.

After dinner, we built up the fire so everyone could feel the warmth; jokes and funny stories warmed our insides. Humor was one more thing bonding us together. Surprisingly, I enjoyed the hunters most. They had the best stories, and they had no pretenses, no "bureaucratic vibes" like some of the Washington visitors.

I grew up in a fishing environment. Fish stories had been passed from one generation to the next, from great-grandfather's spearfishing days to innumerable tales about the big one that got away. The hunters reminded me of those relatives—down-to-earth folks with an oral tradition. Maybe they hunted for social reasons, for sport, for extra meat. But I suspect it was simply in their blood.

Bear hunting was down there below habitat loss and highways as reasons why Florida's black bear population was becoming fragmented and threatened, but I knew then that it would eventually be eliminated because we had the ability to stop it. It is not as easy to halt roads and development in the name of bear preservation.

Under different circumstances, some people in our group might have debated the merits of hunting, especially bear hunting, but they kept silent. It wasn't the time. This was an occasion for the Osceola, for unity. Everyone knew you couldn't hunt bear in a phosphate mine, or hike, or canoe...

Around the fire, Senator Chiles was relaxed, one of the gang, among friends. Earlier that day, however, I had seen him hot with anger. A Forest Service spokesperson stated that the Osceola's total phosphate value could range up to two billion dollars. "If reasonable stipulations are put in," Chiles countered, "I'm convinced this would not be a valuable deposit!" Those stipulations involved restoration on a scale deemed nearly impossible. Sure, pine trees could be planted after mining, and new river channels could be cut and shaped, but then what? What about the diverse array of plant and animal species? How long would it take to restore natural habitats on tens of thousands of acres that took thousands of years to create? Could it be done, and for how much? No one really knew.

When we finally did retire to our cold tents, our quiet Native American looking bus driver kept an all night vigil by the fire. Thanks to him, a warm fire greeted us on the coldest morning in years. The humble driver looked tired but satisfied.

I often wondered about that bit of sacrifice. Only later did I learn about the southeastern Native American practice of keeping a fire vigil during the Green Corn ceremony. Those who stayed up all night by firelight were doing so for all the people, helping to usher in the new year. It was a form of spiritual support.

When I organized a walk across the United States in 1984 in support of environmental sanity, peace and Native American rights, I learned afterwards that a Muscogee Creek matriarch had kept several long vigils for me around a special fire. She never wrote to me during the seven-month journey, never mentioned her vigils, but when a friend told me about it afterwards, I was moved beyond words.

With the bus driver, perhaps his vigil was not only for us, but for the Osceola forest and all that it represented. Silent prayer and focus is the perfect and necessary complement—sometimes the only option—for certain situations. How many mining executives keep an all-night vigil in support of environmental destruction, whether it is a western desert, an Appalachian mountain, or a Florida national forest?

Thanks to many people's efforts that year, the Osceola forest was spared from phosphate strip-mining. When folks unite for a common cause, they can move mountains, or in this case, a strip mine. The victory was also a tribute to a man who personified the idealized role of politician.

Lawton Chiles, the He-coon, was a "down home" man doing uncommon deeds, elevating those around him. In 1998, a month before his second term as governor was set to expire, he died of heart failure. He was one of the few remaining political leaders with deep Florida roots, and he loved the Osceola. In part, due to him, the Osceola forest exists for all the people, in its entirety.

The future holds no guarantees, however. The potential remains for people to be elected or appointed to office—regardless of party affiliation—who have little regard for natural beauty, biodiversity or public lands stewardship. If the need arises, let us hope another He-coon will again walk "just before the light of day."

If You Go

The Osceola National Forest is a vital refuge for Florida black bears, linking to the Pinhook Swamp and Okefenokee Swamp to the north, and to the Ocala National Forest to the south. The 1760-acre Ocean Pond is good for kayaking and there is a Forest Service campground on the north shore. A 20-mile segment of the

Florida National Scenic Trail is a great way to explore the forest. For more information, log onto http://www.fs.usda.gov/detail/florida/home/?cid=LSBDE V3_007320.

32
Cave Camping

In 1969, my scoutmaster, Ken, knew of a deep cave on private property in northwest Florida and arranged for our troop to camp in the cave mouth for a weekend. I was twelve. Just west of Marianna, parent volunteers drove us north of Highway 90 on a muddy, unpaved road through driving rain and dropped us off with our gear at a closed gate, barbed wire in both directions. We slipped through the gate, assuming Ken had received permission from the landowners.

  The property was pocked with chimney caves—vertical shafts that dropped forty to fifty feet before spreading out into an underground cavern. These were inaccessible to us without ropes, but "our" cave had a gaping maw littered with moss-covered boulders. Like generations of native inhabitants before us, we set up camp beneath the broad overhang, enjoying the natural rain shelter and cool air that flowed out of the dark cavern. Soon, smoke hung thick in the air from our cook fires.

  For our cave exploration, we wore old clothes and most of us had "helmets" we made from the bottom of plastic milk jugs. We were a funny looking bunch. Fortunately, no known photos have survived the expedition.

Using flashlights, we explored deep into the cave, marveling at cave formations and side pools of waters. We learned the difference between stalactites—those candle-like formations hanging from the cave ceiling formed by dripping water—and stalagmites—cylindrical formations building up from the cave floor from mineral-laden water dripping on them for millennia. Other striking cave formations were sparkling white calcite "flowstones" that resembled frozen waterfalls, and smooth folds of stone known as draperies.

We could walk upright for almost a mile through the cave, a real luxury since most Florida and South Georgia caves involve long stretches of muddy belly crawls. But to reach the cave's end, we had to drop down into a broad pool of muddy water and then climb a slippery hill to a small room with a low ceiling. Numerous "soda straw" stalactites hung down, a fitting description of their size and appearance. "Now boys, take a souvenir home with you," Ken said as he snapped off a soda straw. Cave conservation was not in our Boy Scout handbook at the time.

I hate to admit it, but we also wrote our initials on the cave walls with Ken's carbide lamp, another cave taboo. As with most graffiti, it was a feeble attempt at immortality. If I could find the cave today and gain access, I would love to do cave restoration, starting first with sanding away the graffiti. Modern Boy Scouts are involved with several graffiti removal projects, such as in Utah's Bloomington Cave. Just as many cave formations took thousands of years to form, some types of cave damage can last for millennia.

On our way back to the entrance, Ken halted our advance and posed a question to us: "Now boys, what would you do if your flashlights died out?"

"Uh, feel our way out?" someone answered nervously. I didn't like where this was heading. I knew Ken.

"Exactly, so we're going to do an exercise. Let's turn off all our lights and find our way out." I thought, how many people jump from a perfectly good boat and swim to shore through unknown and possibly dangerous shark-filled waters? That's how I felt when I flipped off the flashlight beam.

Cave darkness is the blackest experience of all. When outside, even on a new moon, shadows and silhouettes mark the skyline. In a cave, nothing, thus the reason many cave creatures such as crayfish are blind and albino, or, like bats, they use echolocation to navigate. So, we fumbled our way down the corridors, feeling along clammy stone walls and tripping on rocks and stalagmites. Our milk jug "helmets" proved only marginally effective at protecting our heads from protruding stalactites and other obstacles.

At one point, the peeps from flying bats filled the air, prompting one of our scouts, Don, to panic. He screamed and leaped forward, only to strike a large stone column, formed when a stalagmite and stalactite has joined after tens of thousands of years. It came crashing down. We flicked on our lights to find Don sprawled on the cave floor, moaning and holding his forehead. Fortunately, he proved to have no life-threatening injuries, so we continued our dark path to the cave entrance.

If the exercise was a right-of-passage of sorts, perhaps we would emerge from the cave no longer as adolescent boys, but as full-fledged men, ready to embark on broader life journeys with a new sense of confidence. Symbolically, we were moving from the dark abyss of ignorance toward illumination…until the next accident. Once again, a scream pierced the air followed by a loud thud. Flashlights flicked on. A scout had fallen into a deep pit. We helped him climb out, blood streaming from a gash above his right eye. Normally requiring stitches, we practiced our first aid by taping two butterfly bandages over the wound. Soon, the bleeding stopped and we continued toward the cave entrance, this time with our lights on—our journey into manhood indefinitely delayed.

One highlight of the cave campout was Ken's stories. He was a gifted storyteller, whether telling ghostly tales or "Jack" stories of the guy who passed difficult tests and challenges through wit and guile. And with the setting of a campfire in a cave mouth, with constant dripping sounds and eerie echoes when voices were raised, the atmosphere was perfect.

Other Boy Scout troops did more conventional campouts, and we did some of those, too, where we learned knot tying and a host of other skills. But not many scouts ever camped in a cave, or fumbled through darkness, or listened to stories while flames flickered across stone ceilings. Ken wanted to challenge us in ways we would remember, and he succeeded. Many of his ideas would never fly in today's litigious world, but I was glad I was in his troop for that brief moment in time, when manhood was a goal that seemed elusive and mysterious, the journey fraught with peril and filled with magic.

If You Go

These days, the only dry Florida caves of any size open to the public are near Marianna at Florida Caverns State Park. The Florida Park Service offers 45-minute guided tours through thirteen lighted rooms, the only such attraction in Florida. Visitors will marvel at cave features such as the white calcite flowstones in the "wedding room," the rim stone pool that is the shape of South America, and dramatic stone draperies. Cave tours are closed on Tuesday and Wednesday of each week. Call before departing for the park to ensure there are vacancies on the tours, (850) 482-1228. The last cave tour leaves at 4:00 p.m. central time.

The tours are possible through the hard work of the Civilian Conservation Corps of the late 1930s-1940s. For four years, men toiled with hand tools for a dollar a day to open up passageways large enough for visitors to walk through.

The 1,340-acre park also has hiking, biking and equestrian trails, and camping. Paddlers enjoy plying the often clear waters of the upper Chipola River, which runs through the park, and canoe rentals are available. Longer trips on the Chipola River often begin just below the park, http://www.dep.state.fl.us/gwt/guide/designated_paddle/Chipola_guide.pdf. Hiking is popular along the boulder-strewn river bluffs through a floodplain forest noted for several rare plant species. To learn more Florida Caverns State Park, log onto http://www.floridastateparks.org/floridacaverns/default.cfm.

33
When Plans Go Awry: Taking on the Mighty Mississippi

There is a saying that God laughs when we make plans. That's because things beyond our control can quickly alter them. But I'm convinced God has a heartier laugh when our plans are as ill-conceived as the one hatched in 1973 when four inexperienced canoeists decided to set a Guinness world record by tackling the mighty Mississippi River in twenty days—all conceived in Florida 1500 miles away.

      I should have known something was up when Ken, my former scoutmaster and ex-marine, strode up our walkway in Tallahassee carrying a handsome *National Geographic* book about the Mississippi River, America's longest waterway. While leading our scout troop, Ken was well liked and had a knack for creative adventures, such as a survival campout on St. George Island in mid-summer eating only raw oysters (as described in *Waters Less Traveled*) and feeling our way in the dark through a mile-long cave in Marianna (see "Cave Camping" chapter), but none was as ambitious as this latest idea. As Ken sat in our living room with my brother Dave and I, ages eighteen and sixteen respectively, he laid out the adventure while we thumbed through the book, admiring the pretty pictures.

"Growing up in Minnesota, I've always wanted to canoe the entire Mississippi River," he said, "so this summer, I'm going to do it, and because I'm a little crazy, I want to set a world record. To my knowledge, no one has ever canoed the river in only ten days." The ten-day goal was later changed to twenty after further study, but it was still a daunting challenge.

Ken was an easy role model to follow for adolescent boys. He was a muscular, square-jawed ex-Marine with plenty of adventure tales, and he always seemed more comfortable shirtless and in cut-off jeans than wearing nice clothes. Being a self-made type man, he was starting his own concrete business. His Mississippi plan was simple: develop a team of four paddlers, build two custom-made canoes with front seats farther back than normal so a narrow bed could be made to allow paddlers to sleep in shifts, and paddle twenty-four hours a day in order to set a world record. "We'll be in the Guinness Book of World Records," he said. "Are you with me?"

Naive, with visions of Jack London stories dancing in our heads, Dave and I were all in. My parents, not being ones to interfere with boyhood adventures, gave tentative approval, although my dad cautioned, "Now, I know from being in the Army, you can only force troops to march so far before they wear out."

Ken was convinced his shift plan would work—we would not need or even bring tents—and that we would receive adequate rest. He had another young man lined up to be our fourth paddler, a twenty-one-year-old slightly built guy from his church named Vic, so that afternoon, I knew my summer plans would go beyond hanging out with friends and working at the neighborhood convenience store. I was going to canoe more than 2,300 miles from Lake Itasca, Minnesota to New Orleans!

Our gallant Mississippi crew practicing on Lake Bradford in Tallahassee. I'm in the front on left, age 16. Ken Mick is behind me. Vic Johnson is in front on the right with my brother Dave, age 18, in the rear. Photo by Dan Stainer, Tallahassee Democrat, 1973.

The first part of Ken's plan worked perfectly. We found a local guy with a canoe mold who made 17-foot fiberglass canoes and who was willing to customize the seat design. He allowed us to assist, so that kept the price down. We also started training at an area lake, and Ken lined up an interview with the local newspaper. Our mugs were soon splashed across the Sunday feature section:

"Canoeists Take on Mighty Mississippi." In the article, I likened the adventure to that often used cliché "experience of a lifetime." "I'm confident we'll make it," I said.

Ken added, "I used to watch the boats going down the river as a boy, and always thought it would be really something to take the ride myself. Besides, it's a challenge; to me life is doing different things that are challenging."

Soon, nearly everyone in town learned of our gallant adventure, and the story went out on the Associated Press wire service, so relatives in Illinois read about it. Once on the trip, we would even meet people in remote Minnesota cabins who knew about us. We were paddling celebrities who would only rise in stature…or fail like Don Quixote tilting at windmills. The Mississippi River would make or break our reputations. For me, with two years of high school remaining, at stake was a possible prom date with a cheerleading goddess.

Late July found us packing Ken's four door sedan with gear and supplies, our new canoes strapped to roof racks. Ken's wife, Judy, agreed to accompany us since she would have to take the car home after dropping us off. Three people were squeezed in the back seat at all times, making for tight quarters. And on one night, when we couldn't find a motel room, we all slept in the car. Lunch, and a few dinners, consisted of boloney and white bread, or we dipped into our paddling supplies of smoked salami logs, cheese and crackers, pop tarts, nuts and dried fruit, and Tang, an orange drink mix said to be used by astronauts. We did not plan to cook, nor did we bring stoves. Stoves, like tents, were for sissies.

On a crisp morning, we slid yellow canoes into the sparkling 10-foot wide Mississippi River emerging from Lake Itasca in northern Minnesota. Water depth was less than three feet at the lake outlet. Our spirits were high, weather was perfect, and we vowed to see Judy in twenty days in New Orleans. After all, it was the beginning of August and school was to start in about three weeks. Our plan had to work perfectly.

The first sign of trouble came a few hours later. "What's that sound?" I asked Ken.

"I'm not sure," he said.

The roaring grew louder. Soon, after rounding a bend, white water was splashing around the gunnels and I had to kneel in the bow to better push away from rocks as we crashed through rapids. It was an episode repeated every couple of hours since water levels were low, exposing numerous shoals. In between the rapids, the river moved at a snail's pace through wild rice swamps—making huge S-turns—and we dug deeply with our paddles, knowing we needed to make more than a hundred miles every twenty-four hours. We didn't want to fall behind on the first day. But we couldn't speed up the slow-moving river. Was late summer the wrong season for paddling the upper Mississippi River?

Just after sunset, my six hour sleep shift occurred first, but I couldn't sleep. Not with the heat, sunburn, mosquitoes and moving canoe. And then I had to emerge from my prone position to battle through rapids—in the dark. Luckily, our flashlights still worked so I could see the rocks.

By morning, it became apparent that Ken's and my canoe had sprung a leak. The bed was soaked. No problem—we had brought a fiberglass repair kit. When Ken pried open the can, however, it was rock solid. No help there. Used chewing gum mashed into the hole proved marginally effective.

A highlight of the day was a soaring bald eagle, a rare sight in those days since they were still recovering from the ravages of DDT poisoning. The eagle's effortless flight contrasted to our nearly non-stop paddling.

On the second night, thick fog interrupted our progress. I still couldn't sleep much, though, not with the mosquitoes and heat, and the fact that only one person at a time in each canoe could use the "bed." After the trip, Dave recollected, "We had not planned for attempting to paddle in the darkest of conditions even when it was not foggy. Moonlight? Hah!"

By the third night, after crossing several lakes and portaging around dams that day, exhaustion was testing my will and stamina. Dad was right—forced marches were only successful for short periods. My sleep shift began at midnight and I finally conked out. I didn't care if the canoe rocked, or we scraped bottom, or if mosquitoes feasted on my sunburned skin. I slept soundly…until Ken awakened me a couple of hours later, screaming, "Get up, get up, paddle!"

Groggily, I sat up to witness a nightmarish scene of large waves, lightning, and the canoe repeatedly rising and crashing down. In darkness, Ken had guided us into Minnesota's fifth largest water body, Lake Winnibigoshish, and a thunderstorm was hitting. We had no choice now but to face it. Adrenalin filled me as I grabbed my paddle. "Kneel in front!" Ken yelled. "There's too much weight in the back." Vic did the same in the other canoe. Waves rose higher as lightning electrified the air. We may as well have been in the Atlantic Ocean. We aimed for a distant light on the far side of the lake so we wouldn't lose our way. None of the panoramic scenes depicted in the *National Geographic* coffee table book Ken had showed us weeks before could have prepared us. We didn't know it at the time, but Lake Winnibigoshish had claimed the lives of several boaters and paddlers.

  By dawn, exhaustion took hold and we couldn't fight the head wind and waves any more. We allowed the wind to push us to the side of the lake so we could hug the shore in calmer waters. I had never been so worn out, and every time I raised my paddle, the base of my neck felt as though someone was poking it with a hot ice pick. I finally spoke blasphemous words of truth most of us felt but no one wanted to admit, "I don't think we're going to make it to New Orleans by the time school starts, Ken."

  "What?" I knew what he was thinking. I was a quitter. Ken had a well known stubborn streak; once he started something, he would finish it. I did the math for him, calculating our mileage and the time we had left. We were traveling at less than half the necessary pace. No possibility of a world record. The river was too low and slow, our calculations and untried plans dreamed up 1500 miles away in Florida. They had no foothold in reality. Vic and Dave quietly agreed with my assessment, but I was clearly the ring leader in the insurrection. Finally, after much protest, Ken relented. In a day or two, we would reach a bridge of a major highway, he said, and we would have a clear way out. Then, we'd have to figure out how to get home. Judy had returned to Tallahassee. We would be stuck in Minnesota with two canoes and without a ride home.

Even with our realization of defeat, our troubles did not end. We successfully made our way around the huge lake, portaged a dam and reentered the river, but the thunderstorms continued. Lightning was so fierce we were forced to shore, and it continued to rain into the night. Since we had no tents, we stood in the woods cold and wet, shivering, until Vic announced, looking through the birch trees, "I think I see a light." We all looked. We knew we were in a remote area, so a dwelling was unlikely. Still, what if it was a house? A house meant warmth, dryness, maybe hot food!

We walked a ways towards the light, but it always seemed in the far distance. Finally, something told us it wasn't real, just wishful thinking and part of our imagination. Hypothermia was setting in.

We had to do something to improve our situation, so Ken had an idea—make a fire. He instructed us to peel the outer layers of bark from the underside of birch trees since this was the only dry starter material. Once we had a pile, we held a poncho over it to keep it dry and we tried to light it. No luck. Our "waterproof matches" didn't work. I had a lighter, and with help from flammable bug repellent, we were able to start a smoky fire. We fed it through the night, giving us a necessary focus and some warmth. At one point, we began to laugh uncontrollably. "This is the most miserable night of my life!" Dave exclaimed. One by one, we all agreed, laughing loudly with each exclamation. We had gone mad. We even danced a bit, much like the naturalist John Muir in the late

1800s when he danced all night on a frigid mountaintop to stay warm until dawn.

The episode was a lesson: it taught me to laugh when experiencing misery, especially when shared with friends and family. Since then, I have laughed when encountering headwinds and storms while kayaking, camping in freezing temperatures, hiking down mountains in driving rain, stranded along the highway, faced with challenges at work and home, and experiencing sickness. Laughter. It's a great release. The alternative is to be thoroughly miserable, or to travel through life so carefully so as to minimize any exposure to risk. Eventually, however, a spell of misery will likely find you, and you'll be faced with a choice.

After the rainy night, we made it to the bridge and took shelter beneath it through another storm. We pooled our money and Ken and Vic hitch-hiked to the nearest town. They returned with a small U-Haul truck. We stuck the canoes in the back, the sterns sticking out by several feet. While two people drove in the cab, two others had to lie in the canoes in the hot back. That's where those canoe beds came in handy! Still, we joked a lot, even when we had to park the truck in a Holiday Inn parking lot in Louisville because the gas-guzzling truck was rapidly depleting our funds. Pride prevented us from wiring for more money, however, so we sent Vic to Tallahassee by bus to pick up Ken's car. The Holiday Inn manager was kind enough to allow us to use the restroom in the motel lobby, but for food, we chewed on our salami logs for the next three days.

Dave recalled, "That couple days living in the U Haul, I remember working for a few hours helping a man load and unload a truck to move someone, for fifteen dollars. Also, we had some free time, so I hiked up a big hill and got off by myself to do some 'soul searching' and try to figure out how I got myself into this mess! I wanted to get away from the madness. And we had very little money! Ken was vowing the whole time that he would never quit unless he promised himself he would come back and do it. This was a learning experience, or something to that effect."

Once home, after slinking quietly into town without media fanfare, I vowed to never canoe again. I did so only two weeks later. How easy we can forget. To Ken's credit, he did canoe the entire Mississippi less than two years later—in late spring when the water was up—although he brought a tent for sleeping every night. It took him more than two months in a sleeker canoe. His first partner left him in Minneapolis, but Ken was set on continuing. "The only problem I had was my determination to beat the river this time or it would have to kill me," he wrote in his autobiography, *Life is a Great Trip!* "That seems like a high price to pay, but that's just the way I am." Fortunately, Ken found another partner and finished the journey of his boyhood dreams. "I never considered our trip [first attempt] a failure," he concluded, "but rather a learning experience."

After our failed attempt, I switched to backpacking for awhile, whereupon I hiked the Appalachian Trail from Maine to Georgia upon graduating from high school. Although tempted to give up on numerous occasions, I managed to complete the hike along with subsequent long-distance trips. The Mississippi River was a suitable initiation, and a valuable lesson in poor planning.

"That whole episode was the most ill-planned, screwball, wacky, stupid escapade I have ever done," Dave concluded forty years later. "I remember how tired and washed out we all were after the first couple of days and 'reality' started to sink in."

I can still hear God laughing. Although I have paddled numerous waterways since, the Mississippi River was never again on my bucket list.

34
Becoming Curmudgeonly about Life Jackets

"He could have just hit the boat, slapped me with his tail and I'm flipped over in the water. And then we got some issues."
>Kayak fisherman Roger Prouix after hooking a seven-foot shark

Personal flotation devices (pfds), a.k.a. life jackets. Who wants to wear them? They can feel constricting and hot. And they make you look fat. That's a serious mojo killer.

But I'm becoming curmudgeonly about life jackets.

Perhaps my resoluteness was steeled when I was paddling the Kissimmee chain of lakes and Kissimmee River with a small group in 2007. On the third day, we were paddling a shallow canal and stream that connected two lakes. The day was warm, the water calm, and so we took off our life jackets and placed them under bungees behind our cockpits. Florida law says you only have to wear a life jacket if you're under six years of age, so we were still legal.

When we drifted lazily into Lake Hatchineha, we rounded a point and the wind suddenly hit us broadside. We struggled to face our unexpected nemesis as waves lapped around our cockpits. It was a challenge to stay balanced, so turning to retrieve my life jacket was out of the question. How could I be so careless? This was a dangerous situation. As we struggled towards the opposite side of the lake, we were fortunate no one tipped over. I've had similar episodes with prematurely stashing my spray skirt. And so I began to develop a rule through trial and error—just leave the life jacket and spray skirt on, especially when encountering open water and conditions that can rapidly change. As Coast Guard rescuers say, life jackets often make the difference between a rescue and a recovery.

Most outfitters and guides worth their salt require their guests to wear life jackets. Many paddling clubs and associations require participants to wear life jackets on their trips, partly to fulfill insurance requirements. But I often see paddlers on their own not wearing life jackets.

I once joined a highly publicized group of paddleboarders who were promoting a conservation message. Only a friend and I wore life jackets. And with one exception, none of the paddleboarders had life jackets strapped to their boards, defying state law. That's like removing seatbelts from your vehicle. I doubt that most had whistles, either, another requirement.

As we came to shore, film crews and public officials swarmed the boats. Since I coordinate paddling trails for the Florida Office of Greenways and Trails, I took a photo and sent it to the group leader the next morning by e-mail. "Just some friendly advice—for future photo ops, most government entities such as ours require life jackets to be worn for any published photos. Part of our safety message to the public." I felt I couldn't be more tactful, but I received no response.

My colleague Liz Sparks was stronger in her message. "Please don't paddle without a pfd, a waist pack at a minimum!!" she wrote. "We won't be able to publicize your trip if you miss this important item. It is a legal requirement to have one on your board at all times and as a spokesperson for your sport you really need to model safe (and legal) behavior. Good luck out there and please be safe!" No response either.

Liz is another paddling curmudgeon when it comes to life jackets.

You see, people who have positions such as Liz and I are often the ones contacted by media if a paddling accident happens, such as when two fourteen year old boys drowned along Florida's Big Bend Coast in February of 2005. Their school group had embarked from the town of Suwannee in kayaks and canoes for a 4.5 mile paddle to Coon Island along the Gulf of Mexico. A motorized catamaran raft was also in the group.

Choppy water and scattered rains, coupled with inexperience, caused the two boys to become separated in their canoe. The rest of the group managed to tie up to the catamaran raft, even though the motor had conked out. After dark, a chaperone and teenage assistant began looking for the boys, but they also became lost. It wasn't until the wee hours of the morning before the chaperone could place a successful cell phone call. He reached his wife in Georgia, who then notified the Coast Guard. The Coast Guard promptly rescued all members of the group—except for the two missing boys. Their bodies and overturned canoe were found two days later.

A series of poor judgments contributed to the tragic accident. Many in the group were inexperienced paddlers who embarked in poor weather in winter. Some paddled canoes—crafts not normally suited for open water—and they are usually slower than kayaks, so there is a tendency for a group to become spread out. The chaperones didn't know if they had cell service, and they didn't have emergency contact numbers. No one had a VHF radio. Not every vessel had lights, compasses, or GPS units.

I've guided trips for beginners where people have tipped over. While sometimes frightening, none of the situations were life threatening, in my estimation. That's because all of the people wore snug life jackets and once in the water, they were bobbing with heads above the surface, making it easier for me to assist. No one complained about wearing a life jacket then.

Recently, I helped to rescue a more experienced paddler who tipped over in a swift and deep stretch of the Ochlockonee River. Since I was ahead of her, I quickly landed on shore, waded in, and pulled her towards me by the top of her life jacket. It nearly came off, prompting me to grab her slippery arms. After thanking me for saving her life (a bit of an exaggeration), she told me sheepishly that she had loosened her life jacket that morning and unbuckled the bottom strap to be more comfortable. If she had struck her head on the many snags nearby and the life jacket had come off, it could have been fatal.

There have been other instances where people have tipped over and have gotten stuck in muck and hydrilla and if not for their life jackets keeping their heads above water, they might have drowned before being rescued. One outfitter postulated that a major mental hurdle is the legal requirement that only children have to wear a life jacket, giving the impression that adults don't need them.

There are many excuses for not wearing a life jacket—it's too hot, or the water is calm, or I'm a good swimmer. But there can be sudden risks. For example, I've been nearly swamped by powerboats that seemingly came out of nowhere; I once struck a manatee in dark water and it nearly flipped me; I've been nearly tipped over trying to assist a panicked kayaker who had flipped; storms and wind can come up with surprising quickness, as I already mentioned; there can be unseen objects in water where someone can strike their head; I've seen a paddler knocked out of a canoe by an overhanging limb; and there are possibilities of stroke or heart attack.

Then there are spotted eagle rays, sturgeon and other leaping fish that have struck boaters and paddlers.

On a calm Sunday afternoon in the Keys in October of 2010, two kayakers embarked on a lovely paddling trip. Suddenly, a four foot fish leaped out of the water and struck Karri Larson squarely in the chest, puncturing a lung and knocking her out of her kayak. They saw "quite a big fish that was skipping across the water," said rescuer Kevin Freestone of TowBoatUS in the *Sun Sentinel*. "Lo and behold, it went and hit her. Crazy." Some say it was a barracuda, others a houndfish. But the experience landed Larson in intensive care.

Surprises—and accidents—can happen, so it's best to be prepared. Once in the water, especially in choppy conditions or swift current, it can be extremely difficult to put on a life jacket and still keep track of your overturned kayak or canoe, paddle and bilge pump.

The reality is that we can put all kinds of safety advice and information on websites and in brochures, strict laws can be passed, but that doesn't mean paddlers will follow them. It is up to responsible paddlers to keep reminding, nagging, lobbying, cajoling…to become a bit curmudgeonly. One can be a free spirit on the water, and still wear a life jacket.

35
Florida Spirit

Osprey know her as wind. Dolphin as tide. Manatee as spring water. Otter as sheer joy.

For human, she is morning stillness over Florida Bay. Song of birds. Soft sand. Warm sun. Rainbow.

She is Lake Okeechobee, massive and round. The river of grass, unbroken. She is the powerful roar of Suwannee shoals; the sweet coolness of an Apalachicola ravine.

She is panther and deer; bear and manatee; shark and seahorse. Schools of silver fish pulsing as one. She is the whoosh of a dolphin bursting through water and air. She is newly-hatched loggerheads probing an oceanic void.

She is tannin swamp and brackish bay. Pearl white beach and turtle grass meadow. She is thousands of shimmering lakes and waterways that bear human names. She is the alluring eyes of cavernous springs.

She is ancient scrub and longleaf pine. Wiregrass and palmetto. Rattlesnake and black racer. Gopher tortoise, the old sand swimmer. Lightning. Fire. Smoldering lighter stumps. Renewal.

She is the tendrils of grape, the essence of lily. Mangrove, palm and glistening sundew. She is live oak boughs festooned with resurrection fern; renewal after rain.

She is sky on winter nights; animals patterned in light.

She is wing. Raucous rookery. Busy and loud. The buzz of hummingbirds. Cries of red-tails. Echoes of barred owls. Laughs of pileateds.

She is cricket. The cacophony of frogs.

She is mastodon and ivory-bill; temple mound and shell midden; dugout and chickee. She is conquistador hacking through wilderness. She is struggling pioneer. Beleaguered slave. Desperate immigrant. Entrepreneurial dreamer. Starry-eyed visitor. All are alive in her whispers.

She is oyster tonger and poet; stomp dancer and fiddler. She is root cracking through asphalt. She is calm. She is tempest.

She weeps and rejoices, dances and mourns.
She dies, and is reborn.
She is hope.

Bibliography

Adams, Franklin. "The History of Fakahatchee Strand." Friends of Fakahatchee, 2008.

Akin, Edward N. *Flagler: Rockefeller Partner and Florida Baron.* Gainesville: University Press of Florida, 1992.

Anderson, Lars. "Ocklawaha River: The Pulse of Ancient Florida." *The Paddler,* January 2013, http://www.thepaddler.co.uk/expocklawaha.html.

Baker, Mary Frances. *Florida Wildflowers.* New York: Macmillan, 1926.

Balfour III, R. C. *In Search of the Aucilla.* Valdosta: Colson Printing Company, 2002.

Barnett, Cynthia. *Blue Revolution: Unmaking America's Water Crisis.* Boston: Beacon Press, 2012.

Bartram, William. *Travels.* Philadelphia: James and Johnson, 1791; New York: Penguin, 1988.

Belleville, Bill. "Do we want natural Florida to be wild, or kept on a leash?" *Orlando Sentinel,* January 27, 2013, http://www.orlandosentinel.com/news/opinion/os-ed-florida-springs-bill-belleville-012713-20130125,0,6761254.story.

Bemrose, John. *Reminisces of the Second Seminole War.* Gainesville: University of Florida Press, 1966.

Brink, Graham and Justin George and Terry Tomalin. "Trip Paddled into Danger." *Tampa Bay Times*, March 1, 2005, http://www.sptimes.com/2005/03/01/Tampabay/Trip_paddled_into_dan.shtml.

Burt, Al. *Al Burt's Florida: Snowbirds, Sand Castles, and Self-Rising Crackers.* Gainesville: University Press of Florida, 1997.

CMF Public Media. "Bioblitz 2012." May 10, 2012, http://cmfmedia.org/2012/05/bioblitz-2012/.

Corliss, Carlton J. "Building the Overseas Railway to Key West." *Tequesta*, XIII 1953.

Curtis, A.H. "Search for the Torreya Tree in 1883." Report of the Commissioner of Agriculture for the year 1884, Vol 2212, Doc. 178.

Fergus, Charles. *Swamp Screamer.* Gainesville: University Press of Florida, 1998.

Fleshler, David and Juan Ortega. "Leaping Fish Punctures Lung of Woman Kayaking in Keys." *Sun Sentinel*, October 18, 2010.

Giles, Annie L. *Wacissa River Man: The Life and Times of Richard Aron Williams.* Wacissa, FL: self published, 2003.

Jahoda, Gloria. *The Other Florida.* New York: Scribners, 1967.

Keene, Matt. "Flagler Professor Paddles 1,515 Miles, Sets Record." *Flagler College Gargoyle*, January 22, 2014.

Klinkenberg, Jeff. "The Wild Man of Lily Spring." *St. Petersburg Times*, August 13, 2000.

Langston, Reddick. "The History of the Lanston Ferry." CLJ News.com, June 19, 2010, http://www.cljnews.com/20100619the-history-of-the-langston-ferry.

Larson, Ron. *Swamp Song: A Natural History of Florida's Swamps.* Gainesville: University Press of Florida, 1995.

Mahon, John. *History of the Second Seminole War 1835-1842.* Gainesville: University of Florida Press, 1985 (Revised Edition).

Marraffino, Sandra. "The Significance of Lake Rousseau for Wading Birds and Difficulties Encountered During Nesting Season." Marion County Audubon Society, March 7, 2011.

Means, Rebecca and Ryan. "Florida Mainland Remote Spot," http://remotefootprints.org/project-remote/expedition-journals/florida-mainland-remote-spot [accessed 11/29/13].

Mick, Kenneth O. *Life is a Great Trip.* Tallahassee: self published, 2008.

Miller, Doug. "Shark drags fisherman on kayak 4 miles out into Gulf." KHOU.com, August 26, 2013. http://www.khou.com/news/local/Shark-drags-fisherman-on-kayak-4-miles-out-into-Gulf-221239331.html [accessed 1/4/14].

Missall, John, and Mary Lou Missall. *The Seminole Wars: America's Longest Indian Conflict.* Gainesville: University Press of Florida, 2004.

Moran, John. "Reclaiming our Springs." *The Gainesville Sun,* December 29, 2013.

Munroe, Kirk. *Wakulla.* New York: Harper and Brothers, 1885; New York: Grosset and Dunlap, 1913.

National Park Service, Biscayne National Park. "The Joneses of Porgy Key," http://www.nps.gov/bisc/historyculture/the-joneses-of-porgy-key.htm. Accessed 2/27/12.

Nature Conservancy. "Blackwater River State Forest." http://www.nature.org/ourinitiatives/regions/northamerica/unitedstates/florida/placesweprotect/blackwater-river-state-forest.xml. Accessed 1/3/2014.

Pinellas County Department of Environmental Management. "The Weedon Island Story." April 2005.

Prince, Lt. Henry. *Amidst a Storm of Bullets.* Tampa: University of Tampa Press, 1998.

Ray, Janisse. *Pinhook: Finding Wholeness in a Fragmented Land.* White River Junction, Vermont: Chelsea Green, 2005.

Scruggs, Lewis P., "Economic Impact Assessment – Florida Park System." October 22, 2013.

Tebeau, Charlton W. *Florida's Last Frontier: The History of Collier County.* Miami: University of Miami Press, 1957, 1977.

Warnke, James R. *Ghost Towns of Florida.* Boynton Beach: Star Publishing, 1971, 1973.

Washington, Ray. "Jason Gregory's Legacy: House of the Far and Lost." *Gainesville Sun,* 12/12/1983.

Watts, Betty M. *The Watery Wilderness of Apalach, Florida.* Tallahassee: Rose Printing, 1975.

Wilkinson, Jerry, "History of the Upper Keys—Cape Sable Everglades Expedition Draft," http://www.keyshistory.org/CSEE-CapeSableEvergladesExpedition.html [accessed 11/29/13]

Winter, Nevin O. *Florida: The land of Enchantment.*
    Boston: The PageCompany, 1918, 1919, 1921.

Interviews

David Alderson, 2013
Carlos Alvarez, 2012
Daniel Alvarez, 2012, 2013
Dana Bryan, 2013
Clyde Butcher, 2002
Lawton Chiles, 1982
Jim Durocher, 2012
Jodi Eller, 2013
Keith Fisher, 2002
Anna Lee, 2012
Mark Lotz, 2002
Samantha McGee, 2013
Ryan Means, 2011
Mike Owen, 2002
Liz Sparks, 2012
Jim Stevenson, 2013
Ed Watts, 2012
Monica Woll, 2012

Index

A Day Away Kayak Tours, 27, 29
Ackerman, Georgia, *94*, 133, 136
Adams Key, 75
Akin, Deb, 15
Akin, Edward, 15
Alderson, David, 221-231, *223*
Alum Bluff (Apalachicola River), 129
Alvarez, Carlos, 152
Alvarez, Daniel, 149-158, *150*
American Forests, 197
Ames Sink, *115*
Anclote Key, 30
Anderson, Lars, 57-58
Apalachee Indians, 95
Apalachicola Bay, 126-133
Apalachicola Blueway, 137
Apalachicola Bluffs and Ravines Preserve, 167
Apalachicola River, *126*, 126-139, 180-182, 185-187, 238
Apalachicola Riverkeeper, 5-6
Apalachicola RiverTrek, *v*, 5, 126-137
Apopka, 48
Appalachian Trail, 150, 157, 230
Army Corps of Engineers, 133
Atlanta, 132
Aucilla River, 94, 98, 105-106, 108; bottomlands of, 180-182; Half Mile Rise, 101; Sinks, 174-179
Avenue of the Giants (Wacissa River), 93-98, *94*, *97*
Bacon, Francis, 26
Bahia Honda Bridge, 11, *15*

Bahia Honda Sound, 16
Bahia Honda State Park, 12, *15*, 16, 18
Bald Point State Park, 125
Barnett, Cynthia, 132-133
Barren River Canal, 203
Bartram, William, 78
Beard, Dan, 204
Belleville, Bill, 46
Bemrose, John, 54
Big Bend Coast, 5, 76, 83-86, 234-235
Big Bend Saltwater Paddling Trail, 83-86
Big Cypress Bend (Fakahatchee Strand), 204, 206
Big Cypress Bluegrass Band, 80
Big Cypress Swamp, 62
Big Munson Island, 16
Biscayne Bay National Park, 74-75
Blackwater Canoe Rental, 143
Blackwater River, *143*, 143-145
Blackwater River State Park, 144, 145
Boot Key, 10
Boundary Waters (MN), 148, 152-153
Bradwell Bay Wilderness Area, *viii*, 168-173, *171*
Brevard County, 37; Environmentally Endangered Lands Program, 37
Brooks, Hank, 22-23
Brown, Ace, 106
Bryan, Dana, 52, 109-110
Burt, Al, 109
Bush, Jeb, 211
Butcher, Clyde, 205-206
Caesar, John, 56
Caladesi Island, 22

Calusa Blueway, 22
Camp Izard, 55, 58
Canoe and Kayak Magazine, 84
Cape Sable, 99, 102-103
Carr, Marjorie Harris, 61
Castelnau, Count de, 183
Centralia, 185
Chassahowitzka Wildlife Management Area, 185
Chattahoochee, 137
Chiles, Lawton, 208-214, *210*
Chipola River, 142, 220
Civilian Conservation Corps, 220
Clinch, General Duncan, 53-57
Cockroach Bay, 22
Cocoa Beach, 36
Coastal Plains Institute, 99
Coast Guard Auxillary, 9
Crestview, 145
Cross Florida Barge Canal, 60-61
Curry Hammock State Park, 9, 18
Dade, Major Francis, 53
DeKleva, Jim, 44
Deliverance, 47
Desloge, Bryan, 127, 130-131
De Soto, Hernando, 58
Devon Creek, *138,* 138-139
Diaz de Villegas, Rob, 127, 134
Dry Creek, *140,* 140-142
Duby, Jim, 48
Durocher, Jim, 36-38
Eastpoint, 122
East River, 207

Econlockhatchee River, *64*, 64-67
Ed and Bernice's Fish Camp (Ochlockonee River), 119, 122-125
Ellaville, 80
Eller, Jodi, 147-149, *148*
Everglades, 62, 102-104
Everglades National Park, 102, 207
Exum, Jay, 46
Fakahatchee Strand Preserve State Park, *201*, 201-207, *205*
Fanning, Colonel Alexander, 54
Fergus, Charles, 203
Fewkes, J. Walter, 21
Finn, Mel, 203
Fisher, Keith, 198-200
Flagler, Henry, 11, 12-15
Florida Bay Outfitters, 12, 19
Florida Caverns State Park, 220
Florida Circumnavigational Saltwater Paddling Trail, 12, 18-19, 68, 85-86, 156
Florida Department of Transportation, 115-116
Florida East Coast Railway, 12
Florida Fish and Wildlife Conservation Commission, 65, 83, 85, 88
Florida Keys, 5, 8-19, 151, 211, 236; hermits of, 74
Florida Keys Challenge, 11
Florida Keys Overseas Heritage Trail, 14
Florida Keys Over-Sea Railroad, 8, 9, 11-15, 17-18, 99
Floridan Aquifer, 79
Florida National Scenic Trail, 168-173, 176-179, 180, 183, 187-188, 214
Florida Office of Greenways and Trails, 85-86

Florida Outdoor Writers Association, 26
Florida Park Service, 10, 14, 18, 220
Florida Sierra Club, 42
Florida Springs Institute, 58
Fort Brook, 53
Fort Drane, 55-56
Fort King, 53
Fort Taylor State Park, 17-18
Freestone, Kevin, 236
Friends of Wakulla Springs State Park, 118
Gaines, General Edmund, 55-56, 58
Gaspar, Jose (Gasparilla), 74
Ginnie Springs, 70
Gomez, John, 73-74
Grey Eagle Park (Withlacoochee River), 58
Gum Slough, 57
Half Mile Rise (see Aucilla River)
Half Moon-Gum Slough Tract, 57
Hanson, Chad, 66
Harville, Paul, 144
Haulover Canal, 26-27, 29
Hickory Mound Impoundment, 83
High Banks Landing (St. Johns River), 48
High Springs, 71, 77
Hillsborough River, 30
Hines, Jake, 111
Hitchcock Lake (Ochlockonee River), 124
Houder, Charlie, 79
Howell, Bobby, 126
Huey P. Arnold Park (Ochlockonee River), 121
Hurricane Andrew, 75
Indian River Lagoon, 27, 38-39

Inglis, 62
Inglis Lock, 60
Jackson, Andrew, 56
Jonathan Dickinson State Park, 75
Jones, Sir Lancelot, 74-75
Johnson, Vic, 223-230, *223*
Kaufman, Dr. John, 165
Keene, Matt, 68-69
Kelly Park (Rock Springs Run), 48
Key Largo, 9, 12, 14, 18-19
Key West, 9, 11, 12-14, 17-19, 149, 156, 184
Key West Extension, 15, 17
Key West Gazette, 12
King's Landing (Rock Springs Run), 40
Kirkpatrick Dam, 61
Kirkpatrick, George, 61
Kissimmee River, 232-233
Klinkenberg, Jeff, 73
Knight, Bob, 58-59
Knight's Key, 10
Krome, William J., 99
Labor Day Hurricane, 13
Lake Bradford, *223*
Lake Hatchineha, 233
Lake Itasca (MN), 225
Lake Okeechobee, 238
Lake Panasoffkee, 51
Lake Rousseau, 59-60
Lake Tsala Apopka, 53
Lake Winnibigoshish (MN), 226-227
Lake Woodruff National Wildlife Refuge, 42
Langston Ferry site (Ochlockonee River), 120-121

Langston, Reddick, 120
Larson, Karri, 236
Lee, Anna, 152-153
Light, Helen, 129
Lily Spring (Santa Fe River), 71-72
Limpkin, *50,* 50, 87-90, *89*
Lindamood, Frank, 124
Little Big Econ State Forest, 64, 67
Live Oak, Perry and Gulf Railroad (LOP&G; "Lopin' Gopher"), 180-182, *181,* 187
Long Key, 18
Long Key Channel, 9
Long Key State Park, 8
Lotz, Mark, 202-203
Looe Key Reef, 16
Loxahatchee River, 75
Ludloe, Mark, 128
MacDonald, Rod, 17
Mack Landing Campground (Ochlockonee River), 123
Mack Slough (Ochlockonee River), 123, *123*
Manatee Springs, 79
Marianna, 216, 220, 221
Marquesas Keys, 102
Marsh Bend Outlet Park, 51
Means, Bruce, 99, 131
Means, Rebecca, 99-104, *100*
Means, Ryan, 99-104, *100*
Means, Skyla, *100,* 102
Mejeur, Randy, 45
Mellon, Captain Charles, 54
Mendez, Mike, 135-136
Merritt Island National Wildlife Refuge, 26

Mick, Ken, 216-219, 221-230, *223*
Milton, 145
Minnesota, 149, 151-154, 156, 222-229
Mississippi River, 7, 155-156, 221-231
Molasses Key, 12
Money Key, 12
Moran, John, 112
Mosquito Lagoon, 27
Muir, John, 228-229
Munroe, Kirk, 174
Napoleon, 74
Natural Bridge, 89
Nature Conservancy, 129, 167
New Orleans, 225, 227
Newport, 94
Nixon, President Richard, 75
Noss, Reed, 46
Ocala National Forest, 42
Ochlockonee River, *119,* 119-125, 235-236
Ochlockonee River State Park, 124-125
Ocklawaha River, 61
Okaloacoochee Slough, 203-204
Oklahoma (Indian Territory), 51
Oneal, Ben, 122
Orlando, 40, 64
Orlando Sentinel, 46
Osceola, 52-53, 55-56
Osceola National Forest, 208-215
Outlet River, 51
Overseas Highway, 14
Owen, Mike, 202, 205
Owl Creek (Apalachicola River), 138-139

Pacific Crest Trail, 150, 152, 157
Paddle Florida, 8, 18, 41, 50-52, 79, 119-125
Panama City, 75
Panther Key, 73
Parrot, Joseph, 12
Paynes Prairie, 58
Peeples, Grant, 124
Pennekamp State Park, 18
Pensacola, 211
Perry, 76, 92
Pinellas County, 20, 24
Pine Log Campsite (Ochlockonee River), 124
Pinhook River, *105,* 105-108, *107*
Pinhook Swamp, 214
Porgy Key, 74-75
Port Leon, 183-185, 187
Portman, Jennifer, 127, 136-137
Potts Preserve, 51, 57
Prince, Lieutenant Henry, 55-56
Project Remote, 99-104
Prouix, Roger, 232
Rachel Carson Key, 12
Rainbow River, 59
Rainbow Springs, 58
Rathke, David, 58
Ray, Janisse, 192
Reed, Alex, 136
Richards, Bill, 9, 51, 122
Robertson, Chris, (cover photo)
Rock Island, *83,* 83-85, *84*
Rock Springs Run, 40-49
Rodman Reservoir, 61

Rotary Club of Seminole County South, 43
Rum Island County Park (Santa Fe River), 68, 76
Safety Harbor, 22
Sairs, Jon, 16
Sand Mountain (Apalachicola River), 133
Sanders, Jimmy, 122
Santa Fe River, 68-77
Sasso, Tony, 37
Schmidt, Annie, 129
Scott, General Winfield, 56
Sebastian, 193
Sebastian Creek, 198
Sebastian River, 193, 199-200
Second Seminole War, 50, 52-56, 58, 62
Seminole County, 48
Seminole Indians, 50, 52-56, 58, 62
Seminole State Forest, 48
Seminole Wars Foundation, 58
Seven Mile Bridge, 11, *13*
Shelley, Deborah, 43
Sierra Club, 210
Sister's Creek (Keys), 10
Sombrero Beach (Keys), 10
Sopchoppy, 124
Southwest Florida Water Management District, 58
Space Coast Kayaking, 36, 39
Sparks, Liz, 84-86, 234
Spirit of the Suwannee Music Park, 79
Spring Warrior, 75
St. Andrews Peninsula, 75
St. Andrews State Park, 75-76
St. George Island, 221

St. Johns River, 48
St. Marks, 94, 183-184
St. Marks National Wildlife Refuge, 105, 108, 180-184
St. Marks River, 89, 94
St. Sebastian River Preserve State Park, 192-200
Stevenson, Jim, 144-117, *115*
Stout, Jack, 46
Sugarloaf Key, 17, 74; KOA, 16; hermits of, 74
Sullivan, Billy (a.k.a. Shitty Bill), 76
Sumter County, 51
Sun-Sentinel, 236
Suwannee River, 5, 78-82
Suwannee River State Park, 80
Suwannee River Water Management District, 77, 79, 82
Suwannee River Wilderness Trail, 81-82
Suwannee Springs, *78*
Taber, Micheal, 135
Tallahassee, 89-90, 92, 116, 119, 121, 183, 221, 227, 229
Tallahassee Community College, 115
Tallahassee Democrat, 137, 223
Tamiami Trail, 204, 206
Tammerlin (Lee Hunter and Arvid Smith), 16-17, 52
Tampa, 22, 185
Tampa Bay, 20, 21-22, 24, 185
Tampa Bay Sea Kayakers, 22
Tampa Bay Times, 144
Tate, Cebe, 124
Tate's Hell State Forest, 124
Taylor, General Zachary, 74
Ten Thousand Islands, 5, 36, 73-74, 103; Hermit of, 74
Thomason, Mickey, 60
Thousand Islands, *36*, 36-39; Conservation Area, 37;

    Friends of, 39
Timucuan Indians, 58
Titusville, 26
Tollofsen, Theodore ("Teddy the Hermit"); 75-76
Tomalin, Terry, 144
Tonsmeire, Dan, 127
Torreya State Park, 5, 128, 159-167, *159*
Torreya tree, 128, *163*, 163-164
Trapper Nelson, 75
Traylor, Ronny, 124
Tropical Storm Debby, 77
Troy Springs (Suwannee River), *81*
Turner's Fish Camp (Withlacoochee River), 51-52
University of Florida, 72
U.S. Department of Army, 60
Van Dyke, Jesse, 88-89
Wacissa River, *87*, 87-98; Goose Pasture, 95, 98, 101; Slave Canal of, 5, 96, 98
Wakulla River, *4*, *31*, 31-34
Wakulla Springs, 88-89, *112*, 112-118
Wakulla Springs Alliance, 118
Wakulla Springs State Park, 88
Wakulla Springs Wildlife Festival, 111
Wakulla State Forest, 189-191, *190*
Warnke, James, R., 185
Watt, James, 209-210
Watts, Betty M., 93
Watts, Ed (a.k.a. Naked Ed), 68, *71*, 71-73, 76-77
Weeden Island Culture, 21
Weedon, Dr. Leslie, 21
Weedon, Frederick, 21
Weedon Island Preserve, 20-25, *20*, *23*

Weismuller, Johnny, 113
Wekiva Falls RV Park, 49
Wekiva River, *40*, 40-49; Basin of, 45-46; Friends of, 45
Wekiwa Springs State Park, 41-42, 46, 48
Western Sambos Ecological Reserve, 17
Whitehead Lake, 122
White Springs, 82
Williams, Richard Aron, 87, 106
Wilson's Landing Park, 48
Winter, Nevin O., 8, 11
Withlacoochee River (South), 50-63, *62*; Cove of, 53, 62
Woll, Monica, 12, 74-75
Womack Creek Campground (Ochlockonee River), 124
Wysong Dam, 51
Yankeetown, 62
Young, Susan, 26
Zelznak, Rick, 133